DATE DUE

Martin ....
EDITOR-IN-CHIEF

Understanding the Role of Public Policy Centers and Institutes in Fostering University-Government Partnerships

Lynn H. Leverty
University of Florida

David R. Colburn
University of Florida

EDITORS

Number 112, Winter 2000

JOSSEY-BASS
San Francisco

UNDERSTANDING THE ROLE OF PUBLIC POLICY CENTERS AND INSTITUTES
IN FOSTERING UNIVERSITY-GOVERNMENT PARTNERSHIPS
Lynn H. Leverty, David R. Colburn (eds.)
New Directions for Higher Education, no. 112
Martin Kramer, Editor-in-Chief

Microfilm copies of issues and articles are available in 16mm and 35mm,
as well as microfiche in 105mm, through University Microfilms Inc., 300
North Zeeb Road, Ann Arbor, Michigan 48106-1346.

ISSN 0271-0560   ISBN 0-7879-5556-6

NEW DIRECTIONS FOR HIGHER EDUCATION is part of The Jossey-Bass
Higher and Adult Education Series and is published quarterly by Jossey-
Bass Inc., 350 Sansome Street, San Francisco, California 94104-1342.
Periodicals postage paid at San Francisco, California, and at additional
mailing offices. Postmaster: Send address changes to New Directions for
Higher Education, Jossey-Bass Inc., 350 Sansome Street, San Francisco,
California 94104-1342.

SUBSCRIPTIONS cost $58.00 for individuals and $104.00 for institutions,
agencies, and libraries. See Ordering Information page at end of book.

EDITORIAL CORRESPONDENCE should be sent to the Editor-in-Chief,
Martin Kramer, 2807 Shasta Road, Berkeley, California 94708-2011.

Cover photograph and random dot by Richard Blair/Color & Light
© 1990.

Jossey-Bass Web address: www.josseybass.com

Printed in the United States of America on acid-free recycled paper con-
taining 100 percent recovered waste paper, of which at least 20 percent is
postcomsumer waste.

CONTENTS

EDITORS' NOTES

In 1994, Clark Kerr observed, "America now faces, potentially, the most stressful period of interactive relations between higher education and the surrounding society in the more than three and one-half centuries since the founding of Harvard in 1636" (p. xii). Kerr's concern reflected the sentiments of other higher education leaders who worried that declining public resources, greater competition for those resources, and a societal emphasis on economic development posed serious challenges to the traditional role of universities.

Historically, universities have played a unique role in the public life of the United States. From the adoption of the Morrill Act in 1862 and the creation of the land grant university to the present, public universities have been seen as institutions that can assist states and society in addressing a wide variety of needs. How state universities carry out these responsibilities has led to approaches that are as diverse as the universities themselves. Many private universities also developed public policy programs and have struggled with many of the same issues.

The first wave of government-university partnerships commenced at the turn of the twentieth century, when progressive leaders looked to universities to assist them in professionalizing state and local governments. Reacting to the machine politics that had taken control of many local governments and a few state governments, progressives championed efforts to create honest, professional, and well-trained and -educated civil servants.

In the United States, the reform movement took root in Wisconsin under the leadership of Robert La Follette, progressive leader and governor of the state, and the University of Wisconsin, where he had been a student. The so-called Wisconsin model launched the transformation of government by providing education and training for local and state officials and assisting them in identifying issues and problems that would help strengthen democracy and democratic reform in America.

The Wisconsin model captured the imagination of the nation and its universities. Academic leaders oversaw the creation and expansion of departments of sociology, social work, political science, public policy, and colleges of law to further this reform movement. The settlement movement was another offshoot of this academic development. Women and men trained at universities entered immigrant wards to assist recent arrivals in adjusting to American society.

The partnership between government and universities was curtailed in the 1920s, but after the collapse of the nation's economy in 1929, faculty members at many universities joined with political leaders in searching for ways to end the crisis and to help people and governments in need. In New

York, Governor Franklin Delano Roosevelt turned to universities for expertise in addressing the worsening economic situation in the state. Four years later, as president of the United States, he welcomed academic leaders to Washington, D.C., to assist his administration in developing the New Deal programs. Faculty members took leaves of absence to work in government, while others stayed within the university setting and evaluated the new government programs and devised new ways of improving the training of public servants. As the federal and state governments expanded their social services and public works projects, they turned to universities to provide them with the trained personnel to direct these initiatives.

This close relationship between universities and government was occasionally formalized with the creation of university institutes whose purpose was to study public policy and continue to train current and future public servants. These institutes brought together faculty from different departments (most often political science, law, economics, and sociology) who could share their expertise for the betterment of society. During this era, the Institute of Government at the University of North Carolina and the precursor to the Humphrey Institute at the University of Minnesota were established, modeled after the University of Wisconsin, and reflective of the new role that faculty were asked to play in public life.

In these early days, the institutes focused primarily on local and state issues, although individual faculty members were called to Washington to assist at the federal level. The Institute of Government sought to work with public officials to improve North Carolina's state and local government and offer practical scholarship to address public policy issues in the state. With farmers often left destitute by the Great Depression, the Institute of Government became a lifeline to families and governments in great need. In Minnesota, the Public Administration Center, which later became the Humphrey Institute at the University of Minnesota, focused on similar social concerns and on training professional administrators or to address local and state government issues.

World War II saw many academic figures enter military and government service to aid the nation in this time of crisis. In the immediate postwar period, academics remained active in government, advising the Truman administration as the nation adjusted to a peacetime economy and then as it entered the cold war. In the late 1940s and early 1950s, as the cold war heated up, most academics left government and returned to the inner sanctum of the university, disillusioned by attacks on their loyalty by Joseph McCarthy, senator from Wisconsin ironically, and his supporters.

During the 1960s, the second wave of university and college partnerships began. President John Kennedy surrounded himself and his administration with many of the nation's leading intellectuals and academic leaders. The struggle for civil rights reform further inspired many academic leaders and, when coupled with President Lyndon Johnson's Great Society programs, highlighted the need for greater university-government cooperation.

The complexity and longevity of such issues as poverty, racism, hunger, violence, and health care spurred demands for more research by faculty and solutions to these persistent problems. Federal requirements to include the public in state and local program development and implementation also created the need for further university assistance.

The University of Texas at Austin, Northwestern University, the University of North Carolina at Chapel Hill, and the University of Wisconsin responded to these developments by creating institutes or expanding existing ones to fund research, technical assistance, and training. These institutes successfully pursued new funding from the federal, state, and local governments and from foundations to underwrite research in these areas.

In the last two decades of the twentieth century, government budget reductions and the resulting need to ensure that services are delivered in the most efficient and effective way created further demand that state universities assist in new program development and in determining the success of continuing programs. Expansion of government bureaucracies at the state and local levels also created a demand for better-prepared civil servants. During the past twenty years, universities have created such diverse institutes to address these needs. Many of these organizations train large numbers of public servants through master's programs in public administration and public affairs. Several have continuing education programs for state and local officials, and others principally train and educate undergraduate and graduate students for careers in public service.

Each university has, to varying extents, wrestled with internal issues concerning the development and support of policy institutes and programs. The first of these is how to structure the program within the university. While the master's programs fit neatly within the normal activities of academic departments, applied research and personnel training did not. These programs have often found themselves quite removed from the academic core of the university and have struggled to obtain the financial resources and academic and administrative support necessary to ensure their success. Ironically, at the same time, universities have traditionally been committed to public service. Each of the universities referred to in this volume has addressed these issues in different ways. The University of North Carolina, Claremont Graduate University, and the University of Texas have established their institutes as schools within their universities, appointed deans or the equivalent of deans as administrators, and funded full-time faculty positions within the institute or school. By contrast, Minnesota's Humphrey Institute has a small core of tenured faculty and relies heavily on research fellows who must raise their own funds for their research projects. The others use a mix of permanent staff and part-time faculty who are interested in a particular project. All draw on faculty from multiple disciplines who can bring an interdisciplinary perspective and expertise to public policy issues.

The second issue has been how to attract and reward faculty who engage in applied research and training. Traditional academic standards do not reward faculty for either of these endeavors; promotion and tenure are determined primarily by the individual's publication and teaching record, with much less emphasis given to public service. The response to this dilemma has been varied. The institutes that are free-standing academic units and hire their own staff have developed their own systems for promotion and tenure. Others have hired a few key administrative and faculty members and worked with academic departments to allow release time for interested faculty to conduct applied research within the institute and to consider applied research when evaluating the faculty member. The Humphrey Institute's system of fellows who are selected by the institute, but who must raise their own funds for their research and are not considered part of the permanent staff, is a third model.

Each of these models has benefits and limitations. The model in which institutes have their own faculty allows researchers to work full time on public policy issues and be rewarded for their work, and it also provides stability for the program. However, this model does increase the possibility that the institute will not be fully integrated within the academic core of the university, and it can limit the involvement of faculty from the disciplines in policy studies. The time-release model allows flexibility on projects, but there have been problems with finding enough interested faculty to participate and receive support for their research in their departments. Finally, the fellows approach allows maximum flexibility and a mix of practitioners and academic researchers, but places great emphasis on fundraising at the possible expense of projects that have a public benefit, but lack external support.

Each institution has also grappled with the problem of which issues to address. There is never a dearth of public policy issues to study, but funding and faculty research specialties can limit the subject, scope, and duration of projects. In addition, outside political agendas may make some topics inadvisable and some more attractive. To lessen these factors, some universities and institutes such as Northwestern's Public Policy Institute have chosen to focus on a select group of topics or, like the Institute of Government at the University of North Carolina at Chapel Hill, on a specific geographical area. The Rockefeller Institute has opted to select issues that emerge out of the institute's own research priorities. The LBJ School has established a private foundation to support worthwhile projects that cannot be fully supported by other types of external funding. Others have evolved over time more or less according to both funding patterns and faculty interests.

In general, the trend at these institutes has been to focus initially on local or state issues and then, as time and expertise allow, expand increasingly to address national and international concerns. None of these organizations has remained static; each has periodically reassessed its goals and priorities to meet the needs of society or to respond to initiatives from funding sources. Only two of the institutes, North Carolina's Institute of Government and the Reubin O'Donovan Askew Institute at the University of Florida, have retained a focus on issues within their own states. The others are involved in a mix of state and national issues and, for many, international issues. As globalization has increased, so has interest in international developments at these institutes and in examining good government practices in other nations.

By providing a bridge between the public sector and universities, these institutes may offer one of the best answers to Clark Kerr's concern about the survival of higher education in the United States. Over the past one hundred years, they have provided scholarship and training programs that have helped address the needs of the public and private sectors. Their work has been important to local, state, and federal governments in the United States, as well as to an increasing number of countries around the world. These institutes have demonstrated an enduring commitment to public service and to finding effective and innovative ways to address the problems of a changing society.

This volume of *New Directions for Higher Education* provides an overview of the wide variety of university programs that have been established to interface with governments. It notes some of the models that have been created and the ways in which they intersect with society throughout the nation at both public and private institutions. Some of the institutions included have a long tradition of public and civic engagement, while others are relatively new to the scene and reflect new directions at private colleges and public universities.

Whatever the size, shape, or age of these institutes, they have provided scholarship and training programs that have been instrumental in improving the public and private sectors. These institutes have represented an enduring commitment to public service and to finding effective and innovative ways to address the problems of a changing society. It is that investment that has enabled these institutes to continue to prosper and develop.

Acknowledgments

Many people contributed to the completion of this project and deserve recognition. We owe great thanks and appreciation to Governor Reubin O'Donovan Askew, who governed Florida so remarkably from 1970 to 1978 and left a legacy of leadership that has shaped the state since. Governor Askew has been an active participant in the shaping of the Askew Institute from its beginnings, and for that, we are very appreciative and grateful. We are also particularly indebted to Lance deHaven-Smith and John Scott Dailey at the Institute of Government at Florida State University, who have supported the Askew Institute since its inception and have arranged funding for most of its activities.

Several friends who direct organizations that have worked with the Askew Institute over the past few years and facilitated its success also deserve our considerable thanks: Wendy Abberger of Leadership Florida, Rod Petry and Mark Pritchett of the LeRoy Collins Center for Public Policy,

Jon Mills of the Center for Governmental Responsibility, Charles Pattison of 1000 Friends of Florida, Richard Foglesong of Project Governance at Rollins College, and Neil Crispo of Florida Tax Watch. We also thank Lynda Keever, publisher and CEO of *Florida Trend Magazine,* Ann Henderson, and Ralph Lowenstein, who have contributed significantly to the shape and direction of the Askew Institute.

We extend our final thanks to the chapter authors, who put up with our incessant nagging and our heavy editorial hand, and to our editor, Martin Kramer. Our deepest appreciation goes to our spouses, Dale Campbell and Marion Colburn, who put up with our many hours on this project. We dedicate this issue to them in no small appreciation for their support and for enhancing our lives.

Lynn H. Leverty
David R. Colburn
Editors

Reference

Kerr, C. *Troubled Times for American Higher Education: The 1990s and Beyond.* Albany: State University of New York Press, 1994.

LYNN H. LEVERTY *is associate director of the Reubin O'Donovan Askew Institute at the University of Florida and a member of the university's political science faculty.*

DAVID R. COLBURN *is director of the Reubin O'Donovan Askew Institute at the University of Florida. He is also provost of the university.*

1

The emergence of public policy institutes at universities begun with the Wisconsin idea, and the program has continued to be a pioneer in its state, national, and international programs.

Wisconsin Ideas: The Continuing Role of the University in the State and Beyond

John F. Witte

The Wisconsin idea, which symbolically links the University of Wisconsin with the community it serves, has been in the lexicon of American education and politics for over one hundred years. Although there is no strict definition for the phrase, it has a certain meaning for this university and includes the following components: (1) to provide advanced education to as many of its citizens as possible; (2) to create, invent, nurture, and implement new discoveries and ideas that benefit "the commonwealth"; and (3) to use the expertise of the university for the direct benefit of citizens and institutions. The Wisconsin idea dates to John Bascom, president of the University of Wisconsin from 1874 to 1887. The name postdated the activity. With the publication of Charles McCarthy's *Wisconsin Idea* in 1912, the words became symbols for an important purpose and commitment.

The title of this chapter makes the phrase plural to signify the multiple meanings that have always been associated with the phrase and, more important, to signify a transition in its meaning from the decades before World War II to its current formulation. Although there have been changes in the structure and practice between the university and the community, the underlying commitment of Wisconsin ideas still flourishes and will continue to expand. To explain the evolving relationship between the university and its expanded commonwealth requires an understanding of the changing shape of the university, the changing structure of governments, and the current configuration of an economy and society that is at once local, national, and international.

Origins: 1874–1914

The University of Wisconsin began in 1848 as a state land grant university, designed to provide both advanced education to the mass of Wisconsin citizens and education and service beyond its walls to the community. Initially it was a preparatory school, primarily for schoolteachers. Its first president, John Lathrop (1850–1859), expanded the curriculum to include science, literature, the arts, and a department for the theory and practice of elementary education. Although the institution grew and functioned admirably through its first three decades, the university's connection to political and social problems of the state and nation did not occur until John Bascom became president in 1874.

Bascom came from Williams College in Massachusetts, where he had developed a decidedly conservative, laissez-faire-oriented philosophy of political economy, a subject he taught with relish. His attitudes were connected to strong Christian beliefs, and he was active in the temperance movement. Once at Wisconsin, however, his laissez-faire beliefs radically changed. In part to justify state intervention in prohibition, but also in reaction to the monopoly trusts and the great disparities in wealth and income that resulted from the industrial revolution, he slowly but deliberately embraced strong state action and responsibility for ensuring the public good.

Bascom connected his political beliefs to his Christian faith, emphasizing the moral responsibility of institutions and individuals for the common good. In 1887, in a famous baccalaureate address, "A Christian State," he affirmed a clear role for individuals, including students and faculty, to aid their fellows and community. But he also described a set of obligations for the state: to support an income tax, redistribute wealth, and heavily regulate business, especially trusts and the railroads. To answer those who opposed his views on the grounds that they threatened individual liberty, a position he himself held several decades earlier, Bascom replied: "Liberty stands for the use of powers, not their abuse. . . . If we allow the individual to seek what he regards as his own liberty without relation to that of others . . . the commonwealth itself crumbles away and is at length dispersed to all winds of heaven."

Those whom Bascom taught and appointed to faculty positions created what became known as the Wisconsin idea. Among these people were some of the most influential leaders at the university and in government. Students Robert M. La Follette and Charles Van Hise, who in later years linked the university and government in a progressive partnership, were classmates in Bascom's early classes. Professor Richard T. Ely, who came from Johns Hopkins to be dean of a new School of History, Political Science, and Political Economy, was attracted to Wisconsin by Bascom.

La Follette and Van Hise allied later as governor and president of the university, respectively. La Follette ([1911] 1960) wrote of Bascom's influence on him in his autobiography:

> His addresses to the students on Sunday afternoons, together with his work in the classroom, were among the most important influences in my early life. It was his teaching, iterated and reiterated, of the obligation of both the university and the students to the mother state that may be said to have originated the Wisconsin Idea in education. He was forever telling us what the state was doing for us and urging our return obligation not to use our education solely for our selfish benefit, but to return some service to the state [p. 13].

Charles Van Hise was trained as a geologist and, shortly after becoming the first recipient of the doctorate from the university, made major theoretical advances in the field. He became chair of the Geology Department and was appointed president of the university in 1903, three years after La Follette, his friend and classmate, was elected governor of Wisconsin. Van Hise soon abandoned his scientific research to pursue his interests in politics, economics, and social issues. His writing, teaching, leadership of the university, and political activism focused on the excesses of the industrial revolution and its consequences for society. This work led him to support and foster many of the pieces of social legislation that were enacted during and shortly after La Follette's six-year period as governor. Van Hise also encouraged similar work in the most relevant departments in the university.

One of those departments, Political Economy (changed to the Department of Economics in 1918), was headed by Ely. Bascom had been attracted by Ely's book, *The Labor Movement,* as early as 1886 when he wrote to Ely stating how much he agreed with his arguments. Ely's book was influenced by a strong tradition of European socialist support of labor unions and the right of workers to strike. Although Ely did not hold these beliefs for his entire career, they were very pronounced from the time of his appointment in 1892 to 1906, and they influenced a series of academic appointments that followed and then formed the core of the most important department carrying out the progressive agenda as laid out by La Follette and his successors.

During the critical period from 1885 to 1914, the Wisconsin idea took three general forms, all of which continue to this day. The first were extension activities, which moved the knowledge and expertise of the university out into the community. The extension idea, which emerged during the presidency of John Bascom, actually had originated in British universities. At Wisconsin, it was first applied in the area of agriculture, with the creation of "farmers' institutes" in Hudson, Wisconsin, in 1885. These institutes, which consisted of daylong "classes" held in local communities, were rigorously limited to technical farming issues, with discussions of politics and religion strictly forbidden. In the first year, fifty thousand attended. Agricultural short courses, which still exist, began in 1886, with farmers usually coming to the university for more in-depth classes than had been possible in the institutes. Under the leadership of Presidents Thomas Chamberlain (1887–1892) and Charles Adams (1892–1901), these activities were strengthened. Similar institutes were tried in the industrial sector, as exemplified by the "mechanics institutes," but they were less successful.

The second and third forms of the Wisconsin idea involved activity with the state government. Establishing state-empowered commissions to regulate a wide range of economic and political activity was considered at the time as important as direct enactment of legislation. Commissions, established by statute or constitutional provision, were meant to institutionalize the states' power to control and regulate economic entities and issues that had not been subject to state intervention. They were based on the theory that citizen experts could regulate and adjudicate disputes between private enterprises and citizens and recommend state legislation in such areas as taxation, general industrial activity, insurance, and rules and regulations overseeing railroads and utilities.

Although the railroads and the trusts behind them were considered the most important target of regulation, the first state commission, established in 1899, was the Wisconsin Tax Commission. Shortly after came the Railroad Commission (1901), the Public Utilities Commission (1907), the Insurance Commission (1907), and the Industrial Commission (1911). These commissions were created with the aid of university professors, and many faculty members later served as commissioners. John R. Commons wrote the legislation creating the utility and industrial commissions, and he was a member of the latter for a number of years. Professor Thomas Adams was integral to the creation of the tax commission and served for many years as a commissioner. Students of Commons, Edwin E. Witte and Arthur J. Altmeyer, also became members of the Industrial Commission.

In concert with progressives led by La Follette and subsequent progressive governors James O. Davidson and Francis G. McGovern, the university faculty members were instrumental in proposing precedent-setting legislation for the country. At the behest of La Follette, Commons wrote one of the first state civil service laws in 1905 and was involved in drafting the first constitutional provision for workers' compensation in 1911. Thomas Adams was the principal author of the nation's first income tax, also in 1911, which became a model for the nation's first income tax in 1913.

What made all this activity possible was a combination of personal relationships and the resolve of a dedicated and committed group of experts who believed deeply in the service of their state. The personal side of relationship was never more exemplified than in the ties between classmates La Follette and Van Hise. On the eve of La Follette's unsuccessful run for the presidency in 1924, he spoke of his relationship to the university and especially to Van Hise:

> Our University in the early and formative years of Dr. Van Hise's presidency was in a unique and very fortunate position. Governor La Follette and Presi-

dent Van Hise were not only close personal friends but were in complete harmony regarding the fundamentals of public policy and especially regarding the relation of the University and the State. Thus Governor La Follette not only put the "Wisconsin Idea" into operation by means of administrative organizations like the Railroad Commission, but he also enlarged its scope by bringing the University and its faculty into active cooperation with public life [Curti and Carstensen, 1949, p. 132].

These men were clearly idealists, schooled in the moral philosophy espoused by Bascom and the political and economic philosophy of Bascom, Ely, Van Hise, and Commons. That philosophy promoted an active state role in supporting community efforts to build the commonwealth, supporting the average person, and combating what the university men viewed as the evils emanating from the industrialization of American society.

But they also brought something else: the knowledge and expertise that had been enriched by graduate education. They were among the first to receive the doctorate in the United States, certainly in the Midwest. Commons and many of his students not only understood legislation and the legislative process, but they also participated in all aspects of the legislative process, including the creation of some of the most important laws written in the United States at that time.

Going National: 1914–1956

One of Commons's doctoral students was my grandfather, Edwin E. Witte. He, along with his lifelong friend and colleague, Arthur J. Altmeyer, and several of his students, Wilbur Cohen and Robert Lampman, are symbolic of the next phase of the Wisconsin idea: the expansion of the mission to the national level. Witte and Altmeyer had considerable experience in Wisconsin before they went to Washington to work on social security. They were both Commons's students and had been members of the Industrial Commission. They also worked on a number of related legislative projects, including unemployment, disability, and pensions.

In 1934, one year after being appointed as a full professor at the university, Witte was asked by Secretary of Labor Frances Perkins to become director of the Committee on Economic Security. That committee had the responsibility for drafting the Social Security Act, which was signed into law on August 14, 1935. As the key person who drafted and shepherded legislation through a challenging maze of committees and legislative hearings, Witte came to be known by many as the father of social security, a title he never used or acknowledged.

Accompanying him to Washington was Wilbur Cohen, a recent graduate of the University of Wisconsin and one of his students. Another Wisconsin Ph.D., Arthur Altmeyer, who was then an assistant secretary in the Department of Labor, joined them in Washington. Cohen was Witte's aide and assisted the committee. He continued to work in Washington after Witte returned to Wisconsin. For the next three decades, he worked in Washington in the Social Security Administration or the Department of Health, Education, and Welfare (HEW) and rose to become secretary of HEW. In his early years he worked with Altmeyer, who became a member of the Social Security Board. Together Cohen and Altmeyer collaborated for two decades to expand social security coverage and benefits.

Witte continued his work in labor relations and the development of social policy. In the former role, he became director of the National War Labor Board in Detroit from 1943 to 1944, which was responsible for maintaining labor rights and peace during World War II. The board was staffed by so many Wisconsin people that Mark Ingraham later wrote, "Wisconsin-trained economists were so numerous in the War Labor Board that it was reported that you could empty its offices by yelling down the hall, 'To Hell with Wisconsin'" (Bogue and Taylor, 1975, p. 49).

A final example of the Wisconsin idea in this era was the work of Professor Robert Lampman, who received his doctorate under Witte and Selig Perlman in 1950. Lampman's career focused first on the distribution of wealth and income and later on poverty. Following Lyndon Johnson's famous call for a war on poverty in 1964, Lampman applied for and won a federal grant to establish the Institute for Research on Poverty in 1966. He became the first director of the institute, which remains a premier research organization at the university, analyzing poverty in all its related dimensions.

But by the time the Poverty Institute was created, an era in economics, and the Wisconsin idea, had ended. In his presidential address on December 28, 1956, in Cleveland, Witte acknowledged the passing of institutional economics and was highly critical of the abstract mathematical theorizing that replaced it. He feared, correctly, that this new scholarship had little chance of influencing public policy.

The Transition

The experience of the Poverty Institute also symbolizes one of the important transitions in the practice of the Wisconsin idea. A number of post–World War II changes in the university and the government had a dramatic impact on the working relationship between the university and the state. First, both institutions became much larger and more sophisticated. In earlier years, university professors were asked not only to provide ideas for new legislation, but also to draft the legislation. One reason was that they were trained in law and legal matters, but another was that the government had few staff members and could not afford to hire lawyers who had such experience. By contrast, there are ten staff members in the capitol today who draft legislation for the legislature and the governor. And there are few professors with these requisite skills.

The private sector in the state also changed. Wisconsin was a state built on agriculture and dairying, machine tools and other mechanical industries, food processing, and beer. The university greatly aided agriculture, perhaps more than it did the industrial and food processing sectors. But all of these economic sectors have declined and now account for a much smaller percentage of the state's economy. They are being superseded by business services and high-technology industries, which are more closely connected to academic developments at the university.

The changing organizational structure of the university also affected the Wisconsin idea. As departments and disciplines became the center of the university, they responded not only to the university and state needs, but also to the professional norms that defined their specialty. That meant that nearly all disciplines moved from applied to theoretical work, and often to research that involved sophisticated scientific, mathematical, and statistical techniques. The former development made rewards for faculty working on applied problems less attractive; the latter made it more difficult for research to be understood by nonspecialists and more difficult to be implemented as ideas, programs, and policies.

University rules for tenure also changed, as did department and discipline norms. Publishing became much more important, and teaching and service less. "Publish or perish" became the academic standard and remains the norm today. Thus, for example, members of the Poverty Institute, all of whom have appointments in disciplinary departments, are expected to work on such practical problems as poverty and also use econometric techniques and be current on theoretical issues.

These trends have fundamentally altered the Wisconsin idea. With many more highly trained personnel and much more information, the state began to use the university in different ways. Elected officials and appointed bureaucrats, with much better education, staff, and information, relied less on the university to provide an agenda, promote policies, or be involved in their implementation. Rather, they needed more sophisticated ideas, arguments, and evidence. In addition, to bolster arguments in partisan environments, "objective," "nonpartisan" analyses became valuable in political debates. On both scores the university remains an excellent resource of expertise.

The relationship with the private sector has probably changed the most. Early on there was a bifurcated connection. Progressive legislation was probably best characterized in modern terms as antibusiness. Bascom, Ely, La Follette, Van Hise, and Commons shared a hatred of trusts, large corporate power, and the wealth of corporate owners. They also supported labor and the right of labor to unionize in order to have an equal seat at the table with corporations and government.

The animosity of the university toward business has clearly diminished, and that has changed the university-business relationship. As the university produced ever more sophisticated scientific knowledge, partnerships between business and the university grew from the initial connections between biology and dairy to encompass many of the disciplines in the university. Computer science, engineering, biomedical research, chemistry, the Business School, the Industrial Relations Research Institute, and the La Follette School of Public Affairs, to name just a few, began to work with corporations and nonprofit organizations. Many links that were established in the earlier period would have been viewed with suspicion by progressive reformers.

Just as government and private business evolved, so did the university. Seeking tenure and advancement, professors in some disciplines and departments still produced research that was critical to business and government. For example, researchers in the Poverty Institute were able to provide estimates of labor market participation of those receiving (welfare) subsidies in an experimental setting, and still make numerous advances in the way such experiments should be run and in their utilization of statistical analysis. Both policy and academic needs were met.

However, many disciplines followed their own paths, which have increasingly distanced them from the public and private sectors. Economics shifted to mostly theoretical, highly mathematical research; political science became less concerned about policy, administration, and law; and history became so narrowly focused that it lost its public audience. Thus, the academic demands and culture were redefined and shifted faculty away from practical policy problems.

The creation and transformation of the professional schools and professionally oriented departments and institutes filled the void. These included, among others, the Robert M. La Follette School of Public Affairs, the Department of Urban and Regional Planning, the Industrial Relations Research Institute, the Business School, the School of Library and Information Sciences, the Nursing School, the Medical School, the School of Pharmacy, and many departments in the College of Agriculture. These programs, which trained professionals in their respective areas, naturally became aligned with institutions that employed their students.

These activities bring the faculty in close contact with government and business, and that often leads to research, outreach, and consulting relationships. To cite examples from the La Follette School of Public Affairs, the faculty are conducting research on welfare reform, pension and aging programs and reform, educational reforms (school finance, vouchers and education choice, and class size reduction), the state economy and economic forecasting, problems of gangs and youth violence, and environmental issues. One senior faculty member has headed up the governor's commissions on campaign finance reform and on state and local relations.

Although the relationships between the university and the state have changed considerably compared to the earlier period, activities and connections are probably more numerous and much broader across the community. A recent study by the Office of Outreach Development, relying on a survey of 888 faculty, highlighted the extent of outreach activity at the university. Of those responding, 87 percent indicated they had participated in outreach activities in the previous two years. The primary activities broke down as follows: 72 percent gave speeches or presentations, 51 percent served on advisory boards, 48 percent wrote for the general public, and 43 percent conducted research for public or private organizations.

Carrying On

What we have now are Wisconsin ideas. There is no simple idea that fits a slogan on the ways this university relates to the rest of the state. The linkages now extend from the university to state government agencies, private companies, nonprofit organizations, and the international community.

The models, or ideas, for these relationships are varied. In recognition of the research interests of the faculty, external organizations increasingly are willing to provide funding for research of mutual interest. This of course carries with it a number of complications. Will the research lack objectivity because of the source of funding—that is, will the funding source expect a certain result? It also presents problems in terms of who will benefit financially from the research if it ends with products or outcomes of commercial value. But these problems can be solved. The external peer review process for publications in professional journals provides a check on research quality and objectivity. And contractual arrangements, dividing up the benefits of research between the researcher, sponsor, and university, have become the norm in research leading to commercially viable and patentable products.

The current practices of Wisconsin ideas increasingly extend beyond the state and the nation. At times these reflect state interests abroad, such as helping Wisconsin businesses extend their products to foreign markets, as has been done with genetically engineered crops and animals. At other times, state agencies work closely with foreign agencies to share ideas and innovations, with university faculty often providing the expert linkages required. On occasion these contacts simply involve the extension of university knowledge to governments in developing nations or nations in transition. For example, the university's Land Tenure Center has extensive experience in land reform in Latin America and Africa, and faculty there are now extending their knowledge to emerging democratic regimes in Central Europe and the former Soviet states. In another example, a faculty member in La Follette and the Department of Agriculture and Applied Economics has been applying his extensive knowledge of local finance in the United States to reforms in South Africa. Carrying on the Wisconsin idea no longer means applying it simply within the state or the nation, but clearly beyond.

Finally, as communication technology continues its revolutionary journey, the possible contacts with the world beyond the walls of the university promise to expand dramatically in number and form. Interactive distance learning, in both degree programs and other forms, will make more contact possible. The Internet is already the primary form for displaying research. For example, as I write, a major report on a symposium held by La Follette on sweatshops and living wages in the apparel industry is being released instantaneously on a Web site created explicitly for that conference. This report will be forwarded and reproduced so fast that by the end of the week, one hundred messages reporting its Web site existence may lead to thousands of people across the country and the globe downloading and commenting on the report.

Thus, by whatever measure we use and by making simple projections based on already existing technology and methods, Wisconsin ideas are not only secure, but are expanding in important new directions.

References

Bogue , A. G., and Taylor, R. (eds.), *The University of Wisconsin: One Hundred and Twenty-Five Years.* Madison: University of Wisconsin Press, 1975.

Curti, M., and Carstensen, V. *The University of Wisconsin: 1848–1925.* Madison: University of Wisconsin Press, 1949.

La Follette, R. M. *La Follette's Autobiography.* Madison: University of Wisconsin Press, 1960. (Originally published 1911)

For Further Reading

Cohen, W. J. "Foreword." In T. F. Schlabach, *Edwin E. Witte: Cautious Reformer.* Madison: University of Wisconsin Press, 1969.

Ferrick, J., Geisler, M., Shapiro, K., and Sloan, M. *Faculty Outreach: Activities and Attitudes.* Madison: Office of Outreach Development, University of Wisconsin, 1999.

Lampman, R. J. "Introduction." *Social Security Perspectives: Essays by Edwin E. Witte.* Madison: University of Wisconsin Press, 1962.

Lampman, R. J. *Economists at Wisconsin, 1892–1992.* Madison: Board of Regents of the University of Wisconsin System, 1993.

McCarthy, C. *The Wisconsin Idea.* New York: Macmillan, 1911.

Schoenfeld, C. "The 'Wisconsin Idea' Expanded, 1949–1979." In A. G. Bogue and R. Taylor (eds.), *The University of Wisconsin: One Hundred and Twenty-Five Years.* Madison: University of Wisconsin Press, 1975.

Witte, J. F. *The Politics and Development of the Federal Income Tax.* Madison: University of Wisconsin Press, 1985.

JOHN F. WITTE is director of the La Follette Institute and professor of political science and public affairs at the University of Wisconsin.

2

Since the 1930s, the Institute of Government has been a leader in educating and training elected and appointed officials.

The Institute of Government at the University of North Carolina at Chapel Hill

Michael R. Smith

The Institute of Government was founded in 1931 by a visionary law professor, Albert Coates, who perceived a need to close the gap between government as taught in books and government as practiced in real life. Coates saw public officials come into office without government experience and learn on the job as best they could—and at the end of their terms equally inexperienced public servants replaced them. The result was a government that operated largely through local custom. This lack of professionalism and limited institutional improvement meant that citizens suffered because their government was ineffective and inefficient. The mission of the Institute of Government, then and now, is to improve the lives of North Carolinians by working with public officials to improve state and local government. It reflects a belief that elected and appointed officials, once properly informed, will act responsibly in carrying out their duties and obligations.

Albert Coates and his wife, Gladys, made heroic efforts during the early days to finance and operate the Institute of Government. In addition to using their own money, Coates persuaded many of North Carolina's corporate leaders to provide financial support that paid the institute's first staff members and supported its earliest training schools, a monthly magazine, services to the legislature, and research projects. Private support also financed the Institute of Government's first home, a building that was dedicated in 1939. Local governments provided the first public financial support by paying membership dues at the rate of one-half of one cent per city

NEW DIRECTIONS FOR HIGHER EDUCATION, no. 112, Winter 2000 © Jossey-Bass, a Wiley company

and county resident. The institute finally was brought into the university in 1942, a transition that included its first state appropriation in 1943.

Universities include public service as a significant component of their mission, and often consider it as important as teaching and research. Nevertheless, for most of them, public service has a lower status than traditional teaching and research and receives correspondingly fewer resources and less administrative support. Still, many universities remain committed to some level of public service. Higher education resolves this tension between the demand for public service and its distance from the academic core through the creation of specialized structures, largely centers and institutes. These structures permit a university to engage in the important work of public services, but the structure—that is, the center or institute—has a separate and lower academic status, thus preserving the core work and resources of traditional schools and departments.

The history of the Institute of Government reflects this tension involving public service units, but it also departs from the classic pattern in a unique and significant way. Fitting the institute into a traditional university framework presented many challenges. In what was the most significant of many decisions, the institute was granted the academic status of a school, its director was treated as a dean, "and its staff members became faculty members with all their rights and privileges." This departure from the usual academic pattern for public service units placed the institute in a circle closer to the university's traditional core. The result has been a hybrid unit that successfully straddles the academic fault line between public service and traditional scholarship.

Mission

The mission of the Institute of Government is to improve government in North Carolina by engaging in practical scholarship that assists public officials in the areas of law, finance, management, and public administration. A distinctive feature of the institute is the generally comprehensive scope of its work, covering all three branches of government and addressing nearly every level of official within each branch.

The institute's specialization on the government of a single state has enabled its faculty members to understand the unique challenges facing North Carolina's public officials. Coates encouraged faculty members to visit government offices, talk with officials about their concerns, learn their practices and customs, and understand deeply their day-to-day work. The result has been highly relevant teaching, writing, and advising that recognizes differences across North Carolina and offers not generic assistance but assistance tailored to specific needs. As a part of the academic community, the Institute of Government also carries out its obligation to advance general understanding about government and share that information with practitioners and other scholars.

Most of the institute's activities directly benefit public officials, but some faculty activities result in indirect benefits as well. Faculty members respond to inquiries from members of the news media who are struggling to understand issues facing North Carolina government and occasionally offer short courses on such topics as budgeting and open meetings law. Faculty members also respond to inquiries from private citizens who simply want to know more about their government. For example, does it have the authority to take certain action, like the annexation of their surrounding community? The institute promotes good government in North Carolina by helping members of the news media and the general public better understand the duties and responsibilities of their state and local officials.

Institute of Government faculty and staff members must maintain political nonpartisanship and refrain from advocating particular changes in public policy because their overall effectiveness depends on a clear understanding that they will put any personal opinions aside and offer objective guidance. The institute's role is to help elected and appointed officials understand their range of policy options, along with the different consequences associated with each option.

Major Areas of Work and Successful Programs

Faculty members specialize in law, finance, management, or public administration, and they carry out the institute's public service mission through teaching, writing, and advising for public officials within their area of specialization. The full-time responsibility of institute faculty is to focus their academic expertise over time on meeting the needs of North Carolina public officials, not traditional undergraduate or graduate students.

The following example shows how faculty members fulfill the institute's mission. A faculty member who is a lawyer might specialize in one or more of the following legal fields: education, social services, mental health, public health, land use, elections, employment, purchasing and contracting, criminal justice and courts, or taxation. A person who specializes in the field of public health law, for example, works directly with county health officials and their counterparts in state government. The faculty member learns as much as possible about North Carolina public health law, as well as its relationship to relevant federal law. Within the field of public health, the faculty member offers continuing education courses for health directors, public health nurses, and board of health members; a topic might be the law governing the confidentiality of health records. The faculty also engage in research and writing on subjects of interest to public health officials, like a careful analysis and interpretation of a newly enacted communicable disease law. The most common form of advising public health officials is responding to specific telephone inquiries—perhaps a call from a public health nurse asking about the law governing a minor's consent to treatment—but it also could include working with a legislative study commission on a comprehensive revision of North Carolina's public health laws.

Within their academic fields, institute faculty members typically work closely with state and local officials who share the same substantive field. They get to know those officials and their concerns, and a faculty member may work with many of the same officials over the course of many years. This special relationship over time promotes trust, continuity, and credibility and provides faculty members a deeper understanding of local practice and greater insight into emerging needs, which strengthen all of the institute's services.

Teaching. The Institute of Government sponsors more than 230 classes, seminars, schools, and specialized conferences in Chapel Hill and at other sites across North Carolina. It teaches more than fourteen thousand state and local officials each year about their legal obligations, state-of-the-art management techniques, and ways to ensure fiscal soundness for their offices. Course materials are original and specific to the needs of each class. Many programs are designed to orient newly elected or newly appointed officials; others provide continuing professional education for veteran officials over the course of their careers. The following programs illustrate some of the teaching at the Institute of Government.

Schools for Newly Elected Municipal and County Officials. One of the Institute of Government's most important recurring schools is a three-day orientation specifically designed for each group of newly elected local officials. North Carolina municipalities elect new mayors and council members in odd-numbered years, and counties elect new commissioners in even-numbered years.

Each year following local elections, the institute offers its orientation for newly elected officials at multiple regional locations around the state. The school provides an overview of core government functions that new officials must understand in getting started, such as budgeting, personnel, and the division of responsibility between elected officials and their appointed manager. They also learn about important governance issues, including how to work effectively with other board members who have different perspectives and priorities. Each school is cosponsored as part of a longstanding partnership with a statewide professional association—the North Carolina League of Municipalities or the North Carolina Association of County Commissioners. The three organizations work closely together to improve North Carolina government, though in different ways, and the associations look to the institute for the training of their elected and appointed officials.

Municipal and County Administration Course. The municipal and county government course covers core governmental functions and includes information about various line functions. It is a 150-hour course offered in multiple sessions over eight months, designed for city and county officials who want a comprehensive understanding of local government. A competitive application process produces a class of more than one hundred students from diverse government backgrounds (for example, county managers, city engineers, and clerks to governing boards) and from all parts of North Carolina. In addition to a broad geographical representation within each class, the selection committee seeks a mix of large and small jurisdictions.

The course work includes extensive readings and quizzes with each session, and it culminates in a series of long case studies that permit the students to synthesize their knowledge of local government by working together in small groups. The students learn not only from institute faculty members and guest instructors, but also from each other by sharing their experiences and expertise. Graduates of the course have formed an alumni association and, in close cooperation with institute faculty, sponsor an annual update seminar.

Judicial Education Programs. In 1998 the American Bar Association's Judicial Division honored the Institute of Government for its continuing education programs for district court judges and magistrates. Faculty members specializing in courts and criminal justice offer orientation programs for new judicial officials—magistrates, district court judges, superior court judges, prosecutors, and public defenders. They also offer an intensive one-week school for magistrates specializing in small claims cases, for example, and they participate in planning and teaching an eight-day juvenile certification course for district court judges.

One reason for the Institute of Government's success in judicial education has been its ability to build institutional partnerships that advance its mission. All of its training for judicial officials is based on an agreement with North Carolina's Administrative Office of the Courts (AOC), the state agency responsible for administering the court system. This close partnership helps to ensure that the institute understands the latest instructional needs of court officials, and it identifies the institute as the organization primarily responsible for judicial education in North Carolina. Much like its relationship with the North Carolina League of Municipalities and the North Carolina Association of County Commissioners, the institute's close relationship with the AOC aligns it in a partnership with the organization responsible for improving the administration of justice in North Carolina.

Publications. Faculty members extend their education efforts through a variety of institute publications. Each year the Institute of Government publishes and markets more than fifty new books, bulletins, and issues of journals. The institute itself publishes most faculty manuscripts, but a number are published by other governmental agencies, professional journals or by outside publishing houses.

Popular Government. The Institute of Government's longest-running publication is its quarterly journal, *Popular Government.* Begun in 1931 with an issue that examined crime and punishment and governmental reorganization, it continues today with a circulation of eight thousand that includes governmental officials, lawyers, businesses, nonprofit organizations, and

private citizens. Faculty members and others write on topics of current public interest, always with the aim of making public issues accessible to a
broad audience. Most issues contain a mix of articles covering topics like
court security, charter schools, privatization, and local government on the
Internet. When justified by the importance of a compelling public issue,
such as the growing Hispanic population and its implications for state and
local government, the magazine may focus all of its articles on an in-depth
treatment of that subject.

Legislative Reporting Service. In every session of the North Carolina
General Assembly, Institute of Government law faculty members compile
and interpret legislative activity in a publication, the *Daily Bulletin.* The
institute started this service in 1933 because the legislature had little or no
systematic machinery for keeping its members in touch with the content of
bills introduced during the sessions. Faculty members analyze and sum-
marize each bill and all adopted amendments and committee substitutes.
These concise summaries are printed in the *Daily Bulletin* at the end of each
legislative day and are delivered to legislators early the following morning;
fax and e-mail versions are delivered daily to subscribers throughout North
Carolina. These reports give legislators and thousands of state and local officials a manageable way to keep informed about the progress of bills. At the
end of each year's legislative session, faculty members collaborate on a book
that summarizes and analyzes newly enacted statutes. This summary also is
published on the Web.

North Carolina Crimes: A Guidebook on the Elements of Crimes and *North
Carolina Laws of Arrest, Search, and Investigation.* These two publications
illustrate the Institute of Government's long tradition of providing practical
guidebooks for public officials. They meet the challenge of making complicated material accessible to a broad audience without a corresponding loss
of complexity. *North Carolina Crimes* analyzes and explains the legal elements of North Carolina's criminal offenses. *North Carolina Laws of Arrest,
Search, and Investigation* offers an in-depth treatment of the laws regulating
the arrest, search, and investigation of criminal suspects, which necessarily
also covers federal constitutional law. Each book synthesizes large bodies of
appellate case law in ways that are orderly and understandable, and each
offers innovative and original insights into the law. These complementary
publications provide meaningful day-to-day guidance for law enforcement
officers, magistrates, prosecutors, defense attorneys, and judges.

Advising. One of the services that the Institute of Government offers
to North Carolina public officials can be characterized as advising, but in
many cases the advising turns into long-term applied research and writing.
Within their areas of academic expertise, institute faculty members are available by telephone and e-mail to offer advice and assistance to state and local
officials. It is not unusual for faculty members to receive ten or more calls
a day from public officials on different subjects. Many questions can be
answered immediately, but others require research by a faculty member.

North Carolina officials value their ability to receive fast and reliable guidance from institute faculty members over the telephone, and this regular contact keeps faculty members in touch with the challenges facing officials in the field. A pattern of similar inquiries on a subject often amounts to an early warning system, and it may prompt a faculty member to offer a seminar on an emerging public issue or to write and distribute a publication on the topic.

The Institute of Government selectively advises government officials on broader issues over extended periods of time. A faculty member specializing in public management has been working with a city on improving its management effectiveness and its ability to identify and respond to citizen needs. Although the focus is on a single local government, the faculty member is sharing the lessons learned with other North Carolina cities and counties, through both publications and other advising. Many of these advising services are provided without charge to state and local government, but if resources are available, the institute will seek compensation for those that extend over a long period of time.

Other Services. The following example illustrates how the Institute of Government is relying on information technology to assist North Carolina government officials.

NCINFO is a twenty-four-hour-a-day electronic information resource on the Internet for anyone interested in North Carolina state and local government (http://ncinfo.iog.unc.edu). Beginning in January 1995, the institute developed its Web site as a way to close the physical distance between institute faculty and public officials. The goal from the outset was to create a dynamic and evolving electronic medium for North Carolina officials—to connect them with institute resources and other information important to their work and to find ways to connect them with one another electronically. NCINFO organizes and creates links to the most important government-related Web sites in one location, so that North Carolina officials can find whatever they might need without having to sort through the overwhelming array of possibilities on the Internet. NCINFO also includes up-to-date information about Institute of Government programs and services. One of the most important features of NCINFO is its listservs and discussion forums that connect groups of public officials with institute faculty members and with one another. A sampling includes municipal and county clerks, information technology professionals, purchasing officials, and government planners.

Organization and Funding

The Institute of Government continues to be a unique academic unit. It is treated as a professional school at the University of North Carolina at Chapel Hill, and its director reports to the provost and is considered a dean. One reason for this unusual arrangement is that its forty-three full-time faculty members have their academic appointments in the institute, and thirty-eight of those are on the tenure track. (The usual arrangement for centers and institutes is for faculty members to hold appointments in home departments and conduct only a portion of their work within a center or institute.) Institute faculty members are appointed to twelve-month contracts because the needs of North Carolina public officials are not limited to a nine-month academic calendar.

State appropriations comprise approximately two-thirds of the institute's financial support, and they fund faculty and staff salaries. As a consequence, institute faculty members generally have had the freedom to meet the needs of North Carolina officials without considering their ability to pay. The remaining revenue for the institute comes from publications sales, registration fees for schools and conferences, and payments from government agencies for long-term advising projects or specialized teaching. Municipalities and counties throughout North Carolina provide annual support for the institute's operations through the contribution of voluntary membership dues at a rate of eight cents per resident. Gifts from individuals, foundations, and businesses round out the revenue stream. These contributions enable the Institute of Government to offer its programs and services at affordably low prices or free of charge. The Institute of Government's total revenue from all of these sources for fiscal 1998–1999 exceeded $8 million.

Future Directions

As the institute looks to the future, it will have to find ways to diversify its funding and diversify its programs for North Carolina officials.

Funding. The Institute of Government must diversify its funding in order to continue expanding its capacity to meet the needs of North Carolina public officials. A 1994 feasibility study of its fundraising potential indicated that the institute could be successful in increasing private contributions, and so the Institute of Government Foundation was created to support its operations and activities. The institute hired a director of development, who has dramatically expanded grant support from private foundations for new programs and initiatives. A number of endowment funds and professorships now give individuals and organizations meaningful ways to support the Institute of Government. This effort to diversify funding marks a return to the institute's earliest roots, when Albert Coates relied on private donations from North Carolina's corporate leaders.

Faculty Fields of Expertise. It is clear that this expanded capacity should not come at the expense of existing services, especially the institute's strong core of legal services. The institute is continuing its traditional work while exploring new ways to improve North Carolina state and local government. It recently added new faculty members with expertise in two areas that are increasingly important to government: public dispute resolution and performance measurement and benchmarking. The institute also added two faculty members to work with North Carolina school boards in the fields of management and public administration, especially school governance.

The most significant expansion came on July 1, 1997, when the institute assumed responsibility for the University of North Carolina at Chapel Hill's master of public administration program. This addition involves the institute more directly in educating the next generation of public leaders. About 60 percent of its graduates work in North Carolina, and virtually every one of them calls on the institute for advice and assistance. The location of the program at the institute provides students with many opportunities to learn about public administration through direct involvement with ongoing institute projects for state and local government.

Civic Education. North Carolina public officials have asked the Institute of Government to address the serious problem that too many young people do not know how government works or how it affects their lives. The Institute of Government is the organizing partner and provides leadership and administrative support for the North Carolina Civic Education Consortium, a group of more than one hundred organizations that are working collaboratively to help young people become engaged citizens. The Civic Education Consortium seeks to introduce firsthand experience into the teaching of civics in elementary, middle, and secondary schools by bringing community leaders into classrooms and involving students in projects that explore issues in their communities.

Local Government Technology. Information technology has the potential to help North Carolina government agencies improve service, increase productivity, and reduce costs. Yet there is a large gap between available technology and its use by local governments. The gap is especially troubling because citizens have rising expectations about their ability to receive government services faster and cheaper through information technology.

The Institute of Government conducted a local government technology assessment in 1996 that identified a critical need for education and training about information technology. A planning committee composed mostly of city and county officials subsequently studied the assessment and unanimously recommended that the institute create a comprehensive program in information technology. This program will be one of the institute's highest priorities in the coming years because it will enable the institute to diversify its services to public officials and build on its existing strengths.

Conclusion

The Institute of Government has been a remarkably successful academic experiment whereby faculty members meet the needs of public officials on their terms, as opposed to fitting the needs of officials into predetermined research agendas. The university supports this unique academic unit because it produces practical scholarship that fulfills its public service mission while advancing knowledge about government. The institute has created a number of new initiatives to advance its mission, but always in ways that respect its traditions and always balancing the needs of the community with the values of the university. Today public universities are struggling to reconcile their commitment to traditional scholarship with their obligation to society. The Institute of Government represents one approach for resolving that tension, and it offers lessons for academic leaders who believe that public service is an important component of a university's mission.

MICHAEL R. SMITH is the director of the Institute of Government and professor of public law and government at the University of North Carolina at Chapel Hill.

3

This graduate school has focused its programs on governance and the development of the greater Los Angeles area.

The Los Angeles Project at Claremont Graduate University: Analyzing Public Policy in an Era of Partnerships

Thomas R. Rochon

Los Angeles is one of a handful of global cities: geographically sprawling, socially and economically diversified, and with needs for urban infrastructure and amenities that are increasing in magnitude and changing in nature as the city grows and develops. It is a city of stark contrasts. On the one hand, Los Angeles is the global center of the entertainment industry and one of the top dozen centers of commercial trade and high-tech development in the world. On the other hand, Los Angeles is a place where goods are bartered on the street in crowded neighborhoods and where English often is a second language. Los Angeles is difficult to grasp, due to both its size and diversity. Against the trend of big cities elsewhere in the country, the population of Los Angeles grew by 15 percent between 1970 and 1980 and by another 17 percent between 1980 and 1990. With a population of 3.6 million and no fewer than 150 different languages spoken in the homes of its residents, Los Angeles poses challenges of governance comparable to those of many sovereign countries. These challenges cut across all major policy areas: education, social services, transportation, housing, and economic development.

The School of Politics and Economics at Claremont Graduate University is in the process of undertaking a long-term examination of the means by which major infrastructural projects in Los Angeles are identified, and the political and financial support for them mobilized. Its Los Angeles Project

NEW DIRECTIONS FOR HIGHER EDUCATION, no. 112, Winter 2000 © Jossey-Bass, a Wiley company

unites the teaching and research functions of the school around issues concerning the planning, approval, and development of major new projects in the city. Because these projects in nearly all cases involve significant partnerships between the city government and the private sector, they are indicative of the kind of public-private collaborations that are likely to be increasingly common around the country.

Policymaking in Los Angeles remains to this day heavily influenced by the ideas of the progressive movement in the first quarter of the twentieth century. The principal legacies of the progressive era are its approach to city government through the honest and efficient provision of public services and a professionalized bureaucracy that provides those services. The legacy in municipal government is one of nonpartisanship and of checks and balances between a variety of institutions. The nonpartisanship of elected offices means that city officials must put together policy coalitions without the benefit of common party ties. Dispersion of power among a variety of institutions complicates this coalition-building activity. It is a governance model developed under the assumption of a relatively integrated and cohesive city population prepared to give clear policy direction to municipal government. It is not a model of governance designed for the diverse and dispersed communities of Los Angeles today.

It is little wonder, then, that reform of the city charter has been sought on a periodic basis ever since adoption of the progressive-inspired charter in 1903. Although there has been constant tinkering with the city charter through the initiative process, the effectiveness of the progressives in putting checks and balances into effect has resulted in the failure of each major effort at reform, including those spearheaded by otherwise popular mayors and civic leaders. The last major revision of the city charter, in 1924, was no more than a refinement of core progressive values, and a charter reform approved by voters in 1999 further decentralized city governance by establishing neighborhood councils. When the progressives wrote the city charter, the political elite of Los Angeles was white, Protestant, and relatively cohesive (even if the population of the city as a whole was not). The decentralized institutions of city government posed much less of a barrier to concerted action at that time than they do today.

The dispersion of political power is echoed in dispersion of people and economic activity within the city. Los Angeles is an odd quilt-work of incorporated towns and independent cities, some of them islands in the Los Angeles sea. Although there is a downtown district that houses corporate headquarters and the city and county governments, the economic and cultural foundations of the city are quite spread out. Los Angeles consists of literally dozens of communities in the city, distinguished from each other by civic traditions, economic base, and ethnicity.

The progressives' philosophy of local government was that "less can be more." A half-century after the progressive revolution, a new movement of tax cutters took a different philosophical route to reach the same conclusion. In 1978, Howard Jarvis and the other sponsors of Proposition 13 made sure that rapidly escalating property values in California would cease to be translated into windfall profits for city and county government. The primary effect of Proposition 13 has been on social, educational, and health services offered by cities and counties. But this measure to restrict the growth of property taxes has also had an effect on the ability of local governments to put together funding for development projects. The resulting reliance on bond issues means that public funding is often not available even for projects on which the political institutions of the city can reach agreement.

The scarcity of resources to undertake infrastructural maintenance and development, an institutional design intended to make it difficult to act in the absence of widespread consensus, and the social diversity and geographical dispersion of the city all make it relatively difficult to agree on major new initiatives. Yet Los Angeles has seen a flowering of public projects over the last two decades. These include the completion of concert halls, auditoriums, and arenas; the development of several new world-class museums; the beginnings of a revitalized mass transportation system; and hosting the 1984 Summer Olympics. The flip side of urban development is urban preservation, and here too Los Angeles has seen an expansion of work dedicated to defining the landmarks worthy of preservation and finding ways of funding preservation efforts.

In a densely populated area, any major development project is going to spark controversy and organized attempts to prevent the project from going forward. Urban preservation and urban development are often at odds with each other, making difficult the formation of a consensus around decisive steps in either direction. With the large number of choke points and veto players built into the city's governance system, one might expect that determined opposition by any group with size and resources may be sufficient to stop a project proposal. This expectation, however, is belied by the number of projects that have been approved, funded, and carried out over the past decade. While one may always claim that the cultural and physical infrastructure of Los Angeles is insufficient to its needs (this holds true especially for its transportation system), it is safe to say that the extent of new infrastructural development in the city over the decade goes well beyond the level one might expect given the institutional, financial, and community obstacles to new projects. The Los Angeles Project of the School of Politics and Economics at Claremont Graduate University (CGU) seeks to understand the conditions that have enabled this blossoming of public-private collaboration for development projects to take place.

The School of Politics and Economics at Claremont Graduate University

CGU's School of Politics and Economics is a private, graduate-only institution that offers master's and doctoral degrees in eighteen fields, primarily in the professions (business, education, information sciences) and the humanities and social sciences. Part of the Claremont consortium of six colleges, CGU is able to draw on a faculty comparable to that of a midsized university. As an institution dedicated solely to graduate-level education, CGU retains an autonomy in the design of its programs that is not generally found in universities that provide both graduate and undergraduate education.

Located at the eastern edge of Los Angeles County, Claremont is a close but nonparticipant observer in the politics of the city. Although there is much to be said for taking a leadership position from within the city itself, as the University of Southern California has done with great effectiveness, Claremont's role of "proximate outsider" creates possibilities that are less available to a major institution within the city limits.

In the 1999–2000 academic year, for example, the School of Politics and Economics undertook a study of the movement to separate the San Fernando Valley (with a population of 1.3 million) from the rest of Los Angeles. The effort to establish a separate city, which would require a division of its physical and financial assets, has been a polarizing issue. Located neither in the valley nor in the remainder of the city, representatives from Claremont have been able to gain access and maintain credibility in a way that might have been more difficult for a university within the city limits.

The School of Politics and Economics consists of two departments (Economics, and Politics and Policy), each with its own faculties and own degree programs at the master's and doctoral levels. Since the two departments were merged into a single school in 1992, however, there has been an increasing degree of intellectual cooperation. Students in either department may elect tracks of study in the other, and it has become especially common for political science students to study micro- and macroeconomics and to take courses from the econometrics sequence.

The level of faculty cooperation and curricular overlap between the Economics and the Politics and Policy departments has been especially beneficial in the public policy programs at the master's and doctoral level. The master of arts in public policy (MAPP) is a long-established program whose alumni work in many of the local, regional, and statewide agencies across California. Creation of the School of Politics and Economics has, however, given the MAPP a new impetus in the economic analysis of public policy. The recent addition of a faculty member interested in how public policy can stimulate business-led urban development has also strengthened the school's ability to participate as a partner in the ongoing analysis of alternative projects and their relative merits.

A key feature of Claremont's public policy programs is the policy clinic, required of all master's students and strongly recommended for doctoral students. Clinics are organized around a specific question of relevance for governance and the quality of life, in either Los Angeles or the nation as a whole. Recent examples of clinic themes related to Los Angeles include the viability of city charter reform, the potential for electric vehicles to reduce pollution in the Los Angeles basin, and the adequacy of transportation infrastructure in the region.

In 1999–2000, a clinic was developed on the issues surrounding the drive for separation of the San Fernando Valley from the rest of Los Angeles. This study, carried out by five students, examined topics ranging from the issues that led to the separation movement to an examination of how the recent establishment of neighborhood councils affects support for separation in the valley. Students in the clinic met with the leaders of Valley Vote, the organization leading the separation drive, interviewed other city leaders about the issue, and carried out a small-scale survey. The students developed a range of experiences in field research as well as getting a firsthand understanding of how a grassroots movement attempts to force its way onto the political agenda.

The Los Angeles Project

The Los Angeles Project builds on the existing template for public policy study, in which research activities, teaching, and personal engagement all intersect.

With Whom Are We Interacting? City government in Los Angeles bears the twin stamps of the progressive movement: decentralization of authority and nonpartisanship of key offices. Key institutions in the city were created in reaction to the domination of local politics by the Southern Pacific railroad, which controlled both major political parties and the city government itself. Kayden (1990, p. 13) refers to municipal reform early in the twentieth century as a "war against the Southern Pacific." The progressive influences in Los Angeles culminated in adoption of a city charter in 1903 that provided for the initiative, referendum, and recall (making Los Angeles the first city to have a recall provision), as well as the establishment of commissions to oversee city institutions and services ranging from the harbor to the police.

The commissions have been a particularly influential innovation since they serve not only to decentralize government but also to weaken the power of elected officials. Each of the nineteen commissions has oversight of a city department, and commissioners can hire and fire their department's general manager. As Banfield (1965) points out, cities elsewhere have typically repudiated this progressive legacy of weak mayor and multiple commissions, bringing departments instead under the authority of the mayor. In Los Angeles, though, the political governance of the city through the City Council is separated from the policy administration of the city through the commissions, which supervise and manage the city departments.

In short, the legacy of the progressive era is a government whose political leadership is dispersed among the City Council, the County Board of Supervisors, and the mayor's office. Sector-specific policymaking powers are further distributed among the commissions and special service districts.

This kind of decentralized authority pattern often leads to balkanized policy-making, with loss of coordination and control on behalf of the city as a whole. Writing in the mid-1960s, Banfield (1965) observed that decentralization had led to an emphasis on city services that the council members could provide for their districts, with a concomitant neglect of citywide issues: "The council and the departments continued . . . jointly to manage matters of interest to the districts, like rubbish collection and street surfacing. Matters that were (or were supposed to be) of city-wide concern—for example, fluoridation of water supplies, urban renewal, civil defense, and planning for the city's further growth—for the most part continued . . . to be ignored" (pp. 84–85). Banfield backed up his criticism by noting that Los Angeles at that time had no mass transit system, no public housing program, and no active urban renewal program. His assessment was that a perspective on citywide issues would never be enacted unless there was first charter reform that would strengthen the mayor as an executive counterweight to the City Council.

And yet, thirty-five years after he wrote these words, Los Angeles has all of the collective goods Banfield had identified as lacking. Moreover, these projects have been carried out with no change in institutional structure and under conditions of public financial austerity far greater than those present at the time Banfield wrote. These projects have for the most part been conducted by means of public-private partnerships. The central purpose of the Los Angeles Project in the School of Politics and Economics is to understand better how such partnerships come about and what sustains them. The project seeks also to reach a better understanding of how reliance on public-private partnerships influences the development agenda in favor of certain kinds of projects and against others.

What Will the Los Angeles Project Do? Decentralization of city government and limitations on public resources have together produced a pattern in which every major development project is put together as a coalition of political forces and private developers (with, in the case of cultural landmarks such as Disney Hall, a significant role for private philanthropy as well). The reliance on public-private partnerships for city projects echoes the organizational pattern of the entertainment industry in Los Angeles. Every major project of a movie studio is a unique confluence of creative and technical talent. A team is assembled to make a movie, using money belonging to third parties. When the movie is made, the team of financial backers, producers, directors, actors, technicians, and crew is dispersed, never to be reassembled in exactly the same alignment.

So it is with the major development projects of Los Angeles. The 1984 Olympics, the downtown Staples Center sports arena and concert venue, and Disney Hall were all created through the mutual support of public officials and private organizations. In each of these projects, the wherewithal to negotiate the permitting and approval process came from the public partners, and the financial means came from the private side. Participation in the substance of the development process—the questions of what, where, how big, and how expensive—came from both the public and private sides.

The pattern is a little bit different in the case of major private sector initiatives, such as the Playa Vista development project proposed for the thousand-acre site of the former Hughes aircraft plant. The Playa Vista development was announced in 1995 as a planned residential community and as the home of Dream Works Studios. Five years later, the project has yet to win approval. In such cases the specifics of the proposal come from the private partner, and the role of the public partner is to assess the utility of the development for the city and then make a decision on how hard or easy the approval process will be.

Public-private alliances for a major urban development project may have a plethora of motives, ranging from city pride to personal affinities (or the lack thereof) between the principals. But much of the rationale for new development initiatives has to do with their effect on growth and development of the city. Claims are made that new facilities like Disney Hall and the Staples Center will revitalize the downtown district by bringing people to the area in the evening. The Los Angeles Olympics was predicated on a bet (successful in the end) that hosting the Olympics could be a surplus-generating activity rather than an expensive ornament of civic pride. Even the 1999 Van Gogh exhibit in the Los Angeles County Museum of Art was justified as a high-visibility cultural event that brings visitors and profits to the community.

Despite the centrality of claims about the economic benefits of various projects, there is remarkably little prospective or retrospective analysis of actual economic impacts. And this is where the School of Politics and Economics plays an important role in assessing the informal partnerships that generate major development proposals. Projects such as the Staples Center, Disney Hall, and the periodic bids to bring National Football League teams to Los Angeles all rest on estimates of economic costs and benefits. The same can be said of proposals for major expansions or updating of such facilities as the Los Angeles and Long Beach ports and the Los Angeles airports.

In the Los Angeles Project, the School of Politics and Economics plans to develop ongoing clinics around specific development projects. Students will be attached as interns to as many of the public sector and private sector partners in the project as possible—for example, city government, county government, and commissions, as well as developers, foundations, and nonprofit organizations. Students will earn credit for their work on these internships, observing the process of project development while applying their analytical skills on behalf of project analyses. In the semester following the beginning of these internships, the school will organize a policy clinic that brings together the interns so that they can learn from each other. The internship will provide students with experiential learning on the segment of the project they are directly involved in; the policy clinic will offer the opportunity to develop an integrated analysis of the project as a whole.

The Los Angeles Project is of great benefit to both students and the city as the competing claims of potential projects are weighed. It also provides a significant opportunity to gain experience and understanding of how public-private collaborations for major projects are created and sustained. At the completion of the first project study, there will be a major conference on campus for the stakeholders in that project and other public and private organizations involved in similar collaborations. The objective of the conference will be to develop and disseminate observations about the key facilitating elements and the primary obstacles in the use of public-private partnerships for urban development.

Conclusion

In the report of her School of Politics and Economics policy clinic of governance in Los Angeles, Xandra Kayden (1990) pointed out that "Los Angeles is a city largely built of private values" (p. 43). This is not a new development. Issues of public versus private control over the utilities and water supply, and of public or private responsibility for the provision of cultural, recreational, and transportation infrastructure, were already prominent in the days of Southern Pacific power in the city. An observation made over fifty years ago rings as true today as it did then: "Thus far no one has ventured to blueprint the twin responsibilities of public enterprise and private enterprise in answering Los Angeles' needs" (Maverick and Harris, 1947, p. 379). The relationship between the public and private sectors is at the nexus of a number of important issues in urban governance.

Public-private partnerships for city development are founded on temporary, informal, and contingent alliances. Such partnerships evade all efforts at understanding in terms of the formal processes of local governance. Indeed, these partnerships are formed largely to avoid the effects of formal institutional arrangements, which in the case of Los Angeles would tend to lead toward policy paralysis and a focus on service delivery rather than infrastructural development.

The kind of learning that the Los Angeles Project fosters is problem centered and mission oriented. Each student in one of the project's clinics will be exposed firsthand to the process of strategic thinking, decision making, and implementation from the perspective of one of the participating organizations. The work of the policy clinic will be to pool experiences in order to develop a multiperspective view on how informal alliances are created and maintained in the course of working through a project.

Although we are drawing on past experience of policy clinics and the study of Los Angeles, the Los Angeles Project will not begin in this form until late in the year 2000. We cannot yet know how its various parts might work out in practice. We do believe, however, that the traditions of multidisciplinary and applied education already well established in the School of Politics and Economics at CGU are the right traditions to bring to an endeavor like this one. Real-world problems are complex and messy, unlikely to be amenable to solution using a single tool or perspective. The Los Angeles Project will be a success if it is able to contribute relevant analyses to the shaping of the city's major development projects, while at the same time giving students a multifaceted insight into how public-private partnerships are built and maintained.

References

Banfield, E. *Big City Politics*. New York: Random House, 1965.

Kayden, X. "The Los Angeles Past as It Approaches the Future." In *Report of a Policy Clinic in the School of Politics and Economics*. Los Angeles: Claremont Graduate University, 1990.

Maverick, M., and Harris, R. "Los Angeles: Rainbow's End." In R. Allen (ed.), *Our Fair City*. New York: Vanguard Press, 1947.

For Further Reading

Saltzstein, A., and Sonenshein, R. "Los Angeles: Transformation of a Governing Coalition." In H. V. Savitch and J. C. Thomas (eds.), *Big City Politics in Transition*. Thousand Oaks, Calif.: Sage, 1991.

Schockman, H. E. "Is Los Angeles Governable?" In M. Dear, H. E. Schockman, and G. Hise (eds.), *Rethinking Los Angeles*. Thousand Oaks, Calif.: Sage, 1996.

THOMAS R. ROCHON is the dean of the School of Politics and Economics at Claremont Graduate University.

4

The LBJ School offers extensive policy research projects to train students and find solutions for local, national, and international problems.

Building Partnerships with Governments: The Experience of the Lyndon B. Johnson School of Public Affairs

Max Sherman, Marilyn P. Duncan

The Lyndon B. Johnson School of Public Affairs opened in September 1970 on a note of innovation. Its graduate program broke away from the traditional political science framework for public policy schools and offered a new blueprint for public affairs education. The program was built around the idea that the best way to prepare students for public service careers is through interdisciplinary study combined with direct experience working with government agencies and officials. The school's founding dean, John Gronouski, was both a government practitioner and an academic: he had been a cabinet member in the Kennedy and Johnson administrations, the U.S. ambassador to Poland, and a high-level state official in Wisconsin, and he also had a doctorate in economics as well as university teaching experience. This blend of the academic and the practical became a distinguishing characteristic of every part of the LBJ School's program: the curriculum included courses in theory as well as courses that took students into government agencies to work and conduct research; the faculty included academics from various disciplines as well as practitioners from various levels of government; and public service programs included an academic publishing program as well as workshops for government officials. Over time this approach proved to be a highly successful

---

Complete information about the academic and research programs of the Lyndon B. Johnson School of Public Affairs is available on-line at www.utexas.edu/lbj/.

NEW DIRECTIONS FOR HIGHER EDUCATION, no. 112, Winter 2000 © Jossey-Bass, a Wiley company

educational and public service strategy, and today the school enjoys a solid reputation in both academic and government arenas.

To say that this approach has been successful, however, is not to deny that it has faced a number of difficult issues. In the early years, the school was isolated from the rest of the University of Texas not only geographically but also philosophically. The subject matter and teaching methods were not academic in the traditional sense, and the school experimented with pragmatic research models that looked more like government task forces than university research teams. The faculty and administration had relatively few ties to other units on campus, choosing instead to establish research and public service partnerships outside the university. This disconnection was accentuated by the school's generous funding base (largely foundation money), which allowed the LBJ School to thrive without depending heavily on state and university support. The positive side of such independence was that the school was able to develop a separate identity and to build strong external networks. The negative side was that the school was perceived by some units on campus as a maverick program with little to contribute to the larger academic community. By the end of its first decade, the school began to take steps to change this perception, but the maverick reputation persisted for a number of years.

Expanding the school's partnerships with other University of Texas (UT) at Austin departments was a slow and sometimes contentious process. Although the first joint degree programs (in law and engineering) were established in the late 1970s, they lacked clear definition and were slow in becoming fully established within the LBJ School. The LBJ School faculty was divided on the issue of creating additional joint programs. Some believed that such programs would detract from the regular master's program and lead to unwelcome specialization, while others welcomed the opportunity to expand program offerings and attract a different group of students. The latter opinion prevailed, and today the school cosponsors eight joint degree programs.

As a result of these collaborative programs as well as a growing number of research and teaching partnerships, the LBJ School is now fully integrated into the university community. The school's role in strengthening the university's ties with government is acknowledged and supported by the university at large, and its public service orientation blends well with the university's campaign to replace the traditional ivory tower image with one that is more community oriented. More than at any other time in the past, the LBJ School is in a position to draw on the strengths of the university while cultivating external relationships that are essential to its research and service programs.

Research Partnerships

Public policy research, unlike many other forms of academic research, is practical by design. To be effective, it must be tied directly to the needs and capacities of those who make and implement public policy. At the LBJ

School, researchers work directly with government agencies and officials, generally through client-based relationships, to identify issues of concern and tailor the research to the agencies' needs. Research teams often include not only faculty members and students, but agency staff as well. These research partnerships provide valuable learning experiences for LBJ School students while making an important contribution to government programs and operations.

Policy research takes place both within and outside the LBJ School's curriculum, with much variation in scope, strategy, and format. Two research vehicles are particularly good examples of how the LBJ School ties together its teaching, research, and public service goals: policy research projects and policy research centers.

Policy Research Projects

The policy research project (PRP), one of the most successful elements of the LBJ School's academic program, is a tremendously effective mechanism for creating productive relationships between the school and governments. A required course in the master's degree program, the PRP is a yearlong research project conducted by a team of one to three faculty members and ten to fifteen graduate students. At least ten projects are conducted each academic year on a range of topics. Because the research is directed toward solving actual policy problems, the goal is to produce recommendations that an agency can use to improve its operations, for example, or information a legislature can use in making policy decisions. Project findings and recommendations are provided through a variety of formats, including published reports, Web pages, staff briefings, workshops, and committee hearings.

In selecting a PRP research topic, high priority is given to developing a client relationship with a policy-oriented organization, generally a government agency. The experience of working on real problems defined by government clients teaches students that research for the purpose of affecting the policy process involves something more than drawing policy inferences from theoretical data. They come to appreciate that persuasive research findings are not likely to bring about policy change unless political realities have been taken into account.

From the vantage point of government agencies, working with PRPs offers several advantages. The projects provide a politically neutral, dependable source of information, and they are considerably less expensive than research conducted by teams of private consultants. Some agencies sponsor projects year after year because they find that working with graduate students and faculty experts is a way to bring fresh ideas and intellectual energy into the planning process.

In most cases policy research projects produce a final report with their findings and recommendations. The LBJ School maintains an Office of Publications to publish these reports, which not only are provided to the client agencies in whatever quantities are called for in the contract, but also are included in the school's Policy Research Project Reports Series. In this way the reports are made available to a wider audience, including other interested agencies and government officials as well as libraries, and have a greater potential impact than if they were provided only to the client. As of the fall of 1999, the series had 135 volumes.

Policy research projects vary widely in their approach, but they share a common purpose: to provide a meaningful educational experience for students along with a useful research product for those in the public policy arena. Some examples show how different projects have accomplished this goal.

Texas State Budget Project. Two faculty members with decades of experience in Texas state government—one a former lieutenant governor and the other a former legislative budget director—led two PRPs on the development of the Texas state budget. The client was the Legislative Budget Board, which prepares the budget for the Texas legislature. The first project, conducted in 1993–1994, developed a computer model that allowed users to create different budget scenarios in order to see how budget choices in one area affected allocations in other areas. The model, named the Texas Budget Simulator, was created by the students in the project with techniques they had learned in their quantitative methods classes. Before the beginning of the 1995 legislative session, every member of the Texas legislature was given a disk copy of the simulator, along with a published report that provided instructions on its use and described some of the political and financial issues that influence the state budget's development. The response by the policymakers was so positive that the two faculty members, along with a staff member from the State Comptroller's Office, directed a second PRP in 1995–1996. The second project increased the scope of the simulator, moved it to the World Wide Web, and tied its use to state and federal revenue trends. Again the response was positive, and the Legislative Budget Board posted the simulator on its Web site during the next budget cycle. A number of students in the policy research projects later went into fiscal management positions in state and federal government.

Transportation Studies Projects. One LBJ School faculty member who is an expert in transportation policy has led a series of PRPs on transportation issues affecting the United States and Mexico in the wake of the North American Free Trade Agreement (NAFTA). The projects began in 1989, six years before NAFTA went into effect, with a request from the U.S. Department of Transportation's Office of International Transportation and Trade for an analysis of Mexico's transportation system. Building on the research gathered during that study, a series of PRPs were conducted over the next six years under contract with the Texas Department of Transportation and the Federal Highway Administration on various aspects of transportation and trade between Texas and Mexico. The reports produced by these projects were widely disseminated to government officials and planners in the United States and Mexico. The Texas Department of Transportation and Federal Highway Administration have continued to fund new studies each year on topics ranging from state rail policies and programs to the Texas waterway system to multimodal and intermodal transportation in the United States, Western Europe, and Latin America. These projects have been popular with LBJ School students interested in economic development issues and regulatory policy, providing rich opportunities for field research and close interaction with public officials at several levels of government in the United States and Mexico.

Colonias **Projects.** LBJ School researchers have had a longstanding interest in policy problems related to the *colonias*, unincorporated residential areas along the Texas-Mexico border. In 1975–1976, a PRP conducted the first detailed study of the *colonias* in South Texas, collecting information about their location, history, and socioeconomic conditions that state and federal officials would use to begin a long process of legislative review and action. A documentary film produced by students in the project to accompany their presentations to government officials later won a national award. In 1989 the Texas Legislature passed the first in what would become a series of bills related to the *colonias*, many of them informed by LBJ School research. Two PRPs funded by the U.S. Department of Housing and Urban Development between 1995 and 1997 produced a three-volume report on the population and housing characteristics that determine public policy toward the *colonias* and the costs of planning water and wastewater infrastructures. The project's preliminary findings were presented during hearings of the Texas Senate Committee on International Relations, Technology, and Trade and became an important part of the committee's deliberations.

In a separate PRP conducted in 1994–1995, a faculty member who served on Governor Ann Richards's task force on *colonias* led a PRP that conducted fieldwork in six *colonia* settlements on both sides of the border to gather comparative information about the politics, economics, and sociocultural processes affecting *colonia* development. Project members organized a major conference that brought public officials from Mexico to share ideas with Texas legislators, community groups, nongovernmental organizations, and researchers. Based on the project's findings as well as his own research, the faculty member wrote a book designed to convince the Texas legislature that previous approaches to the *colonias* situation were counterproductive and that new legislation was needed (Ward, 1999). The professor appeared often before legislative committees in 1998 to discuss his proposals, and the book was adopted by the legislature's Mexican-American Caucus. As a direct result of the arguments outlined in the book, the legislature passed a number of bills in 1999 designed to address some of the problems.

Research Centers and Programs

Like other university graduate schools, the LBJ School attracts outside funding to support a number of specialized research centers and programs. These units, staffed by teams of professional researchers and student research fellows, work with government clients on projects that examine some of the more complex policy issues facing them: the overhaul of a delivery system, for example, or the potential impacts of a new funding mechanism. Two programs provide excellent examples of how this kind of research structure offers opportunities for university-government partnerships.

Ray Marshall Center for the Study of Human Resources. Ray Marshall, a UT Austin economics professor who later served as secretary of labor in the Carter administration, established a research center in 1970 to study issues related to labor, rural development, equal employment opportunity, and other socioeconomic issues. By the time the center became part of the LBJ School in 1987, it had an international reputation for its research not only in those areas but in the areas of education, welfare reform, and health policy as well. Over the past decade, the center, which exists entirely on contracts and grants, has been involved in a number of important initiatives at the federal and state levels. For example, in the late 1980s, it conducted research for the National Commission for Employment Policy that led to provisions included in the 1992 reform of the federal Job Training Partnership Act. Between 1993 and 1995, center researchers produced a series of policy reports on welfare reform that had a direct impact on key provisions of the welfare reform bill passed by the Texas Legislature in 1995. A hundred-page amendment to the bill that provided for the consolidation of the state's workforce development system was also based on research generated by the center. One of the agencies created by the amendment, the Texas Council on Workforce and Economic Competitiveness, subsequently contracted with the center to help resolve some of the implementation issues associated with the consolidation. In 1999–2000 the center is involved in seven projects, including a study of child care subsidy systems, sponsored by the U.S. Department of Health and Human Services; an evaluation of a project for the prevention of secondary conditions among children with disabilities, sponsored by the Texas Department of Health; and a six-state project on urban welfare-to-work transitions for welfare recipients, sponsored by the U.S. Department of Labor's Employment and Training Administration.

U.S.-Mexican Policy Studies Program. Established in 1988 with funds from the William and Flora Hewlett Foundation, the U.S.-Mexican Policy Studies Program is an international research arm of the LBJ School. The program's early focus was on trade relations between the United States and Mexico, with particular emphasis on the NAFTA. Researchers' projections of NAFTA's potential impact on various trade sectors led to their being asked to serve on several state committees and task forces, and their reports were circulated widely among trade economists and planners. They also testified before several congressional committees about the effect of free trade on the Texas and U.S. economies. Recent research and publications have examined such topics as the trade in medical services across the Texas-Mexico border, the new federalist system in Mexico, and water management in the Lower Rio Grande Valley. The program sponsors conferences and seminars that bring Latin American scholars and public officials from both sides of the border to the LBJ School to engage in dialogue on issues of mutual concern.

Professional Development Partnerships

Since its inception, the LBJ School has had an active program of professional development and continuing education for those already working in the public sector. For these professionals—city managers and judges, county commissioners and auditors, state legislators, and agency directors—the LBJ School offers a vital link to new information and strategies.

The Pre-Session Legislative Conference, sponsored by the school since 1971 and now cosponsored with the Texas lieutenant governor and the Speaker of the House, is but one example and serves both as an orientation session for newly elected members of the Texas Legislature and as a discussion forum for returning members. Held biennially between the November election and the convening of the legislature in January, the conference acquaints new legislators with state government operations and House-Senate procedures. A general session for all members is devoted to panel discussions of the major issues facing the legislature in the upcoming session.

In addition to its training programs, the school's Office of Professional Development sponsors a number of special conferences on public issues. The annual Ethics in Government conference brings together state legislators, state agency directors, ethics advisers, and human resource managers to discuss such topics as ethics and leadership, open records and open meetings laws, and dispute resolution. The conference is cohosted with the Texas Ethics Commission. Three national conferences on performance measures have brought government representatives from throughout the country to the LBJ School to examine the latest strategies for using performance-based measurement tools. Conference cohosts include the state offices of the lieutenant governor, Speaker of the House, state comptroller, and state auditor. Other conferences, all cosponsored with government agencies, have looked at such issues as managed health care, social security, technology innovation, and the desegregation of the military.

Public Service Partnerships

The LBJ School is involved in a number of public service programs of particular benefit to government officials and administrators. Among the most interesting of these are the Guatemalan Legislative Modernization Program and the *Guide to Texas State Agencies*.

Guatemalan Legislative Modernization Program. Through a three-year technical assistance program that is helping to consolidate democracy in Guatemala, the LBJ School is participating in a project that will eventually lead to the modernization of the Congress of Guatemala. The program is funded by a $3 million U.S. Agency for International Development grant to UT Austin that involves the LBJ School, the Law School, and the Institute of Latin American Studies. It aims to help the Guatemalan Congress implement the 1996 Peace Accords, which ended nearly forty years of civil war in Guatemala. Two LBJ School students helped write the proposal that won the grant in late 1997. The students then served as the liaison team between the UT Austin-based Legislative Technical Assistance Committee and other Legislative Modernization Program staff in Guatemala. The committee consists of UT Austin faculty members who are experts in such areas as public policy, Latin American studies, law, international trade, and electronic information systems. Working with the LBJ School student team and other graduate students from UT Austin, these experts are training top Guatemalan graduate students to perform such functions as legislative and budget analysis, recodification of the Guatemalan legal code, constituent services and civic education, and staff training. The Guatemalan students typically begin their tenure with the Legislative Modernization Program as volunteers and eventually move into salaried positions within the Congress or other government entities. Over time this corps will strengthen the foundation of Guatemala's democratic government and help ensure its viability.

Guide to Texas State Agencies. Called "the Bible of state government" by the governor's office, the LBJ School's *Guide to Texas State Agencies* is a publication with a long history and an important public service role. First published in 1945 by the University of Texas Bureau of Municipal Research, one of the LBJ School's predecessors, the *Guide* offered the first description of the organization and functions of the state's major agencies. The LBJ School now publishes the *Guide,* producing a new edition every two years to incorporate changes made by the legislature (which meets biennially). The tenth edition was issued in 1999.

The only publication of its kind on Texas state government, the *Guide* has attracted a large following among public officials, agency administrators, librarians, teachers, and other professionals. Despite the fact that most agencies now maintain Web sites, the book still offers the most concise and accessible source of information about programs and functions across the spectrum of agencies.

Other Cooperative Ventures

In addition to the programs already described, the LBJ School is linked to government through activities that send faculty and students to work with government and bring government officials to work with the LBJ School.

Agency Sabbaticals. Acting on a request by the LBJ School, the governor of Texas issued an executive order in 1993 urging state agencies to hire university faculty members on interagency contracts to work on agency staffs for one or two semesters. Both agencies and faculty members benefit from such arrangements, which take the form of paid sabbaticals. The first professor to take advantage of this opportunity was an LBJ School faculty member, who spent one year as a policy adviser to the Texas Transportation Commission. He worked with the three-member commission to reorganize the Department of Transportation and develop a statewide transportation plan. Not only did the agency benefit from his expertise, but the professor returned to the classroom with a renewed understanding of the inner workings of state government.

Officials in Residence. Each year the LBJ School hosts several visiting fellows who spend a year in residence on leave from their sponsoring agencies to exchange ideas and information with students and faculty. These have included Fulbright Fellows from developing countries, a fellow from the Central Intelligence Agency, annual fellows from the European Union, and diplomats-in-residence from the State Department.

Student Internships. As part of the required master's curriculum, students hold twelve-week summer internships, working as full-time paid staff members in government agencies and other organizations with a public policy focus. Internship placements are made throughout the United States at all levels of government—from the Congress to municipal agencies—and in areas of the private and nonprofit sectors. Students also hold internships in a variety of international settings. In many cases these internships lead to job offers.

Partnership Prospects for the Future

Public affairs schools are potentially a university's strongest link between the world of academia and the real world of government. In the case of the LBJ School, this link has always been an integral part of the program's identity and purpose. The school has been fortunate in its location: UT Austin is the state's flagship university and offers a wealth of intellectual resources; Austin is the capital city of Texas and offers convenient access to state government operations; Mexico is the state's next-door neighbor and provides rich opportunities for cooperative research and training. Strong foundation support has allowed the development of new programs as well as the ability to take on PRPs without external funding. The school has also been fortunate in attracting faculty and students with a strong commitment to public service and a desire to build productive relationships with the public sector. With many successful programs already in place and a number of new programs on the horizon, the school is in a position to use these attributes to even greater advantage in the future. The following provide a few examples:

- The increasing importance of the nonprofit sector in the realm of public affairs is creating a new demand among government officials and public policy students for programs that focus on nonprofit management. The LBJ School's new Southwest Center for Philanthropy, Volunteerism, and Nonprofit Management will support a range of initiatives, including a concentration in nonprofit management for students interested in pursuing careers in that sector, a program of research and publications on nonprofits, and community outreach programs.

• A new wave of interest in leadership—not only its relationship to good government but the values that underlie its exercise—is evident in both government circles and the schools that train students for government service. In response to this interest, the LBJ School has established the new Center for Ethical Leadership to coordinate course work, research, and outreach programs in the area of leadership studies. Many of the center's activities will collaborate with government agencies and public officials.

• Technology policy, an interest of LBJ School faculty members for many years, is taking on new dimensions in the era of the Internet and the high-tech revolution. The new Technology and Public Policy Program within the school's Policy Research Institute is expected to increase the numbers and kinds of technology-related projects undertaken in partnership with the public and private sectors.

• Diversity issues are at the forefront of policy discussions in both governments and universities. Attracting qualified minorities into government service is an important part of the LBJ School's mission, and the school supports this mission through its student recruitment program as well as through special activities aimed at promoting diversity in the public affairs arena. One of these activities is the Barbara Jordan Memorial Forum on Diversity in Public Policy, an annual event that brings together current and prospective students with a diverse group of alumni working in the public sector. The forum, established by students in 1996 in honor of the late congresswoman and LBJ School professor, makes an important statement about the school's commitment to diversity in its own community and in the community at large.

Conclusion

The new initiatives point toward an increasing level of cooperation between the LBJ School and its partners in government, with potential benefits that go far beyond the immediate gains for students and government officials. Over time, these partnerships will improve the ability of governments to achieve what President Johnson called one of the most cherished principles of our democracy: the greatest good for the greatest number. The LBJ School remains committed to that goal.

References

Lyndon B. Johnson School of Public Affairs. *Guide to Texas State Agencies.* (10th ed.) Austin: Lyndon B. Johnson School of Public Affairs, University of Texas, 1999.

Ward, P. M. *Colonias and Public Policy in Texas and Mexico: Urbanization by Stealth.* Austin: University of Texas Press, 1999.

For Further Reading

Blissett, M., Schmandt, J., and Warner, D. *The Policy Research Project at the LBJ School.* Austin, Tex.: Lyndon B. Johnson School of Public Affairs, 1979.

Howard, A. "Time of Transition: Schooled for Leadership." *Texas Alcalde,* 1986, *74,* 16–17.

MAX SHERMAN holds the Max Sherman Chair in State and Local Government at the Lyndon B. Johnson School of Public Affairs, University of Texas at Austin.

MARILYN P. DUNCAN has been the director of publications at the Lyndon B. Johnson School of Public Affairs since 1977.

5

The Institute for Policy Research has been a leader in focusing on those at the margins of society and producing interdisciplinary policy research.

Linking Research and Policy Concerns: Northwestern University's Institute for Policy Research

Fay Lomax Cook, Audrey Chambers

The Institute for Policy Research (IPR) began in 1968 as the Center for Urban Affairs with one house, three part-time faculty, a secretary, and a $15,000 research grant. By the year 2000, it was supporting thirty-one core faculty, a research staff of twenty-eight lodged in five campus houses, and over $16 million in grants. Its history has been marked by a commitment to high-quality, policy-relevant research that addresses such societal concerns as poverty, crime, race and inequality, social welfare policy, and community building. The mission of IPR is to stimulate and support social science research on significant public policy issues and to disseminate the findings widely—to students, scholars, policymakers, and the public at large.

The institute's research agenda reflects its belief that research plays a key role, along with ideology and interests, in deliberations about policy decisions and in understanding the process and politics of policymaking. A second guiding principle is that the link between research and education is vital. Students at IPR—both graduates and undergraduates—contribute to the research enterprise.

Founded during a period in the mid- and late 1960s when urban riots swept the United States, IPR initially focused its efforts on improving the quality of urban life, developing an interdisciplinary urban curriculum for students, and creating field studies programs to afford students real-life training. With Chicago as its laboratory, IPR's earliest research projects dealt with such issues as high school dropouts, redlining, determinants of urban

health, citizen responses to environmental concerns, delivery of city services, and the labor market experiences of migrants. Some of these initial
studies were the seeds of major themes that have distinguished IPR research
throughout its history and remain dominant today: racism and poverty,
community development, and criminal justice reform.

The institute owes its longevity and success in no small measure to the
substantial institutional support it has received from Northwestern University for both faculty research and graduate student training, but its ambitious
programs of research would not have been possible without grants from government and private foundations. Although the institute has never had what
IPR faculty would call formal partnerships with either government or foundations, its major research interests have been largely consistent with a select
group of granting agencies that value research to promote the nation's economic, social, psychological, and political well-being and its quality of life.
Perhaps the closest links to a government agency came in the past decade,
when the Department of Health and Human Services funded the Joint Center for Poverty Research (JCPR) in 1996. In many cases, IPR research findings have percolated into the national debate on social policy issues and have
been used to inform the discourse on enlightened public policy.

The history of IPR is inextricably bound up with several major funders
that have supported the institute's most significant streams of research: the
Ford Foundation, the National Institute of Justice, the Chicago Community
Trust and other private foundations, the U.S. Department of Health and
Human Services, the MacArthur Foundation, and the National Science
Foundation.

The Founding of IPR

In the mid-1950s, IPR founder Raymond Mack, a professor of sociology best
known for his groundbreaking work on race, joined with a group of interdisciplinary Northwestern faculty who met regularly as the Center for Metropolitan Studies to work on urban issues. The university formalized its
commitment to this effort in October 1968 by creating the Center for Urban
Affairs to focus an all-university effort on finding solutions to some critical
urban problems.

The Ford Foundation underwrote that commitment in May 1969, and
the funds were designated to support twelve faculty and their research, with
a mandate to promote interdisciplinary urban policy research and training.
With university approval, Mack expanded the number of faculty represented
at IPR by converting the twelve full-time positions into twenty-four half-time
positions, all of them affiliated with university departments. Selected faculty gained half-time release from their respective departmental teaching loads so they could devote time to policy-relevant research. The Ford
grant also provided support for twenty-four graduate students involved in
research projects of the IPR faculty. More than two hundred were supported

during the first decade alone. When Ford's funding ended in the early 1970s, the university assumed financial responsibility for the twenty-four half-time positions as well as the graduate student support. This long-standing commitment by the university administration to support policy-relevant research has helped to maintain IPR's vigor and quality.

From the earliest days of the program, IPR faculty members have conducted field studies in Chicago, Philadelphia, and San Francisco. They have served as masters and associated faculty for the university's Residential College of Community Studies, which IPR faculty helped to found in 1972, and for the university's Public Affairs Residential College, and they designed special urban courses for undergraduates throughout the university. In 1998, the institute began a summer undergraduate training program in statistical research methods that is building a pool of undergraduate research assistants. It plans to expand that program into a year-round effort.

Organization and Structure

IPR has seven research programs and two working groups. The institute has thirty-one faculty fellows who are supported by IPR either quarter-time (releasing them from one-fourth of their teaching load) or half-time (releasing them from half of their course load) and forty-one faculty associates. These faculty members represent sixteen departments in eight of the university's nine schools. They collaborate with research associates, visiting scholars, graduate students, and undergraduates on research projects and participate in conferences, a weekly colloquia series, and workshops. These activities are supported by the university, grants from local and national foundations, government agencies, corporations, and gifts. In 2000, fifty-nine research projects were funded by outside sources, nineteen by government agencies, and forty by foundations.

IPR publishes a research brochure, newsletters, and a working papers series to disseminate faculty research. Abstracts of working papers are posted on IPR's Web site (www.northwestern.edu/IPR), and some working papers are available for downloading. To bridge the gap between the academic and the policymaking worlds, IPR sponsors the Distinguished Public Policy Lecture Series. IPR has hosted lectures by such figures as Donna Shalala, secretary of the Department of Health and Human Services; Paul Simon, former U.S. senator; and David Ellwood, former assistant secretary for planning and evaluation in the Department of Health and Human Services and Harvard professor of public policy.

To fulfill its mission of both stimulating and disseminating research, IPR hosts a range of conferences. For example, in May 2000, the conference titled "Polls, Policy, and the Future of American Democracy" brought together scholars, pollsters, politicians, and journalists to examine the increased role of public opinion polls in American political life. Under the auspices of the Joint Center for Poverty Research, conferences are held that focus on the causes of poverty and the effectiveness of programs and policies to alleviate it.

Relationship Between Social Issues and Funders

Four dominant themes have characterized IPR research since 1968, each with important funding sources:

- Poverty and social welfare, funded by the Ford Foundation, the National Science Foundation, and the MacArthur Foundation
- Inequality and race, funded by the National Science Foundation and the Ford, Spencer, and Mott foundations
- Criminal justice, funded by the Law Enforcement Assistance Administration, the National Institute of Justice, the National Science Foundation, and the Ford and Eisenhower foundations
- Community development, funded by the Chicago Community Trust and the Spencer, Joyce, Annie E. Casey, Kellogg, and MacArthur foundations

All four research programs, each with roots in Chicago, illustrate the evolution of the institute's mission from local urban problem solving to analyzing public policy issues of national significance and contributing to the national debate.

Poverty and Social Welfare. Since its inception, IPR has devoted much of its research to aspects of social welfare policy formation, institutions that implement it, politics, and impact on individuals, families, and communities. Its researchers have explored the social concerns that are most often viewed as endemic to welfare populations but that affect other groups in the United States as well: public housing, unemployment, inadequate public schools, female-headed households, poor health, and the revolving doors of mental institutions. IPR faculty have made concentrated efforts to understand past failures to solve these problems and to help develop feasible alternatives.

Social welfare policy took center stage at IPR in the early 1980s. After President Ronald Reagan's landslide victory in 1980, the welfare state was seen by many to be in a state of crisis—ideologically, politically, and economically—because the president promised to reduce the role of government in domestic life and proposed changes that would dismantle many social welfare programs. In 1986, his director of the Office of Management and Budget, David Stockman (1986), proclaimed that "the Reagan Revolution . . . required a frontal assault on the American welfare state. Accordingly, forty years' worth of promises, subventions, entitlements, and safety nets issued by the federal government to every component and stratum of American society would have to be scrapped or dramatically modified" (p. 8).

Concern about the impact of these new and proposed policies was manifest in an unusual consortium of eighteen Chicago-area foundations, banks, and corporations that funded a collaborative effort by four local universities (IPR at Northwestern, the University of Chicago, the University of Illinois at Chicago, and Loyola) to assess the extent of economic hardship in Chicago during the Reagan administration and to examine its causes. The IPR portion of the study, led by sociologist Christopher Jencks and political scientist Fay Lomax Cook, concluded that the distribution of income had become more unequal during the 1980s. They found that half of Chicago families felt worse off in 1983 than in 1981, and that groups hit hardest by the recession and cutbacks in government programs from 1981 to 1983 were blacks, poorly educated whites, and single mothers. In contrast, college graduates improved their economic standing during the same period (Cook and others, 1986).

This project opened a new line of work that tilted the poverty debate from discussions about measuring income alone to also measuring material well-being. With Ford again providing funding, Jencks and sociologist Susan Mayer began a project to rethink the accomplishments and failures of social policy. They determined that official poverty statistics based on income were misleading because they did not take into account material well-being. They also suggested that analysts may have been misreading the ways in which material conditions changed in the United States after World War II and consequently were drawing erroneous conditions about the effects of social policies aimed at altering these conditions (Jencks, 1992).

In October 1989, IPR cosponsored a national conference to critique and expand on the ideas advanced by sociologist William J. Wilson, then at the University of Chicago, in his landmark book, *The Truly Disadvantaged* (1987). Nineteen papers presented by leading urban poverty researchers in the country were published in the 1991 book *The Urban Underclass*, edited by Christopher Jencks and Paul E. Peterson of Harvard. The authors concluded that the major issue was not so much a growth in the size of the underclass as the persistence of poverty. Furthermore, the most important problem—the rise in the percentage of children living in poverty—was due to the increasing number of female-headed households and the decline in the earnings of young men.

The conference strengthened IPR's ties to the University of Chicago and paved the way for the two universities to create a joint interdisciplinary research-training program for advanced students in race, poverty, and social policy funded by the National Science Foundation. This effort culminated in the 1996 award by the U.S. Department of Health and Human Services that established the JCPR.

JCPR's primary mission is to advance understanding of the causes and consequences of poverty and the effectiveness of policies designed to reduce it. In addition to disseminating current research through conferences, policy briefings, workshops, information sessions, working papers, newsletters, and electronic media, it coordinates a far-flung network of research affiliates, trains graduate students, and seeds new studies by junior scholars and faculty.

Among the many JCPR/IPR projects concerned with welfare reform is a six-year panel study headed by Dan Lewis, professor of education and social policy. It is tracking fifteen hundred former and current Illinois welfare recipients to learn how the reforms have affected their experience in the labor market and their families. Several foundations and the National Institute for Child Health and Human Development combined to support another large IPR project concerned with the effects of welfare reform on children. This $20 million study, codirected by developmental psychologist Lindsay Chase-Lansdale, one of six coinvestigators, is tracking twenty-four hundred low-income families in Boston, Chicago, and San Antonio. One of the study's primary concerns is whether the recent reforms have helped poor families become self-reliant. Ethnographic work also attempts to show the influence of welfare reform on neighborhood resources and state and local child services.

At the same time, economist and JCPR director Greg Duncan, with assistance from four Northwestern graduate students, is examining the effects on children and family functioning of the experimental New Hope antipoverty program in Milwaukee. This program offers cash subsidies and health and child care benefits to poor families who enter the workforce (Duncan and others, 1999).

These three projects demonstrate how poverty and racial issues are so closely tied to the ways in which social programs, policies, and context affect the lives of children, adolescents, and their families. Recognizing these interconnections, IPR has developed a strong nucleus of faculty from Northwestern's departments of communications studies, sociology, and economics and its law and education and social policy schools. Among other issues, these researchers are studying family preservation policies, child protective services, the effects of social contexts on child development and high-risk adolescents, school reform, and links between schooling and the labor market.

Inequality and Race. In its early years, IPR established a research cluster known as the Urban-Suburban Investment Study Group to investigate metropolitan housing programs. Law professor Leonard Rubinowitz led a study of segregated housing that was used by plaintiffs in the U.S. Supreme Court's landmark *Hills* v. *Gautreaux* case in 1976. That decision provided a metropolitan-wide remedy for discrimination in Chicago's public housing. With the help of housing vouchers and support services provided by the Metropolitan Leadership Council for Open Communities, some seven thousand low-income black families have been relocated to Chicago's largely white middle-class suburbs or to better locations within the city. This "natural experiment" in racial and economic integration has been the subject of IPR research since 1981, sponsored by several foundations.

The first of this long series of studies found that the move to the suburbs for the Gautreaux children had been generally positive, and a second study released found that low-income black mothers significantly improved their job prospects by relocating to the suburbs and that families felt safer. Later studies found that significantly more suburban youth were enrolled in college tracks in high school and went on to college, and a higher proportion of youth who went into the labor market had full-time jobs at higher wages and better benefits than those who remained in the city. The program has become a model for similar programs in Boston, Cincinnati, Dallas, and Hartford and inspired the national Moving to Opportunity program in five U.S. cities.

In another major initiative of the Ford Foundation, IPR analyzed how the increasingly diverse populations of major U.S. cities, with large waves of immigrants from the Far East, the Middle East, and Latin America, assimilated with older populations. The IPR team examined four groups of new residents—Laotians, Koreans, Latinos, and New Poles—and three older established ethnic groups—Polish Americans, American Jews, and African Americans—in the Albany Park area of Northwest Chicago. They found that the assimilation process has been traumatic. Much of the population was poor and unskilled, gangs roamed the streets, fear of crime increased, and much of the housing was dilapidated and decaying. Language barriers often interfered with communication, most of the newcomers were left out of the political process, and organizations that might have assisted them were often unknown or out of touch with their needs. The researchers recommended that leaders in organizations and institutions be trained to communicate more effectively across class and ethnic lines and that policymakers strive to strengthen ethnic associations that might serve in a class-mediating intercultural role.

Related to issues of inequality and race, mental health has been another important strand of IPR research. A 1987 report by education and social policy professor Dan Lewis and others found that low-income black males ages eighteen to thirty-four predominated among patients admitted to Chicago-area state mental hospitals and that 97 percent of these admissions were voluntary. His work suggested this was more of an underclass phenomenon than was recognized at the time, that the need for shelter accounted for at least 18 percent of the readmissions, and that the system had failed to encourage former patients to become self-sufficient. The work had particular significance for the debate about the future of mental health in Illinois following two decades of deinstitutionalization.

The Chicago Community Trust and the Illinois Department of Mental Health and Developmental Disabilities supported a subsequent study by Lewis that tracked clients released from four Chicago state mental hospitals. It concluded that deinstitutionalization had made the care and control of the mentally ill far more difficult than it was under the old mental health system, which relied on state hospitals rather than community care for these patients. Lewis, Riger, Rosenberg, and Wagenaar (1991) found that patients were returning to hospitals because of personal problems, conflicts with families, community disturbances, and personal preference and that most did not have criminal records. It recommended that services be spread out into the community and that the link between poverty and the problems of the mentally ill be addressed head on.

Criminal Justice Studies. IPR researchers have undertaken more than two dozen major crime research projects since 1970 through which they have built an international reputation for their work on crime. Traditionally, research on crime and consequent policymaking has concentrated on offenders, scrutinizing their backgrounds and motives, and devising strategies to alter or punish their behavior. Early in the 1970s, however, IPR crime researchers began to treat crime as an interaction among victim, offender, the police, and the environment.

Although local foundations and organizations funded the earliest research efforts, support from the federal government dominated IPR's subsequent crime research. This support reflected the government's growing recognition that America was facing a national crisis in crime that demanded solutions beyond the borders of cities. In the early days, IPR scholars were more closely tied to constituencies in Chicago who proposed topics for research they could use to reform the system. IPR scholars, however, chose topics they wanted to pursue and conducted the research independently of the groups. For example, during the 1970s, IPR published a series of reports that dealt with such issues as trying juveniles as adults, the Cook County Coroner's Office, and the use of fatal force by the police.

During that period, the federal government was concerned with procedural changes to improve criminal justice. At IPR, for example, the National Science Foundation and the National Institute of Mental Health funded projects that dealt with collective violence, corrections reforms, local police procedures, monitoring juvenile delinquents, and teenage drug use.

A major shift in direction occurred in 1975, setting the tone for two decades of IPR crime research when the Law Enforcement Assistance Administration awarded IPR researchers a $1.5 million five-year program project grant to study reactions to crime. Rather than focusing on offenders and police, this study examined victims and, more specifically, the causes and variations in behavioral and psychological reactions to crime. A large team of IPR researchers looked at how the increase in crime since 1964 had affected ten neighborhoods in San Francisco, Chicago, and Philadelphia. The results pinpointed neighborhood conditions that generated fear of crime and revealed that people in high-crime areas often do less to protect themselves than those in lower-crime locations, in part because of their relative inability to organize collectively (Lewis, 1981).

But IPR's director, Margaret Gordon, and psychologist Stephanie Riger found an important and overlooked aspect of this research: the effects of fear, and especially fear of rape, on women. As the feminist movement was gaining strength in the nation, the federal government responded by creating the National Center for the Prevention and Control of Rape within the National Institute of Mental Health. That new center granted funds to Gordon and Riger for a related study that examined how women's day-to-day behavior is affected by the fear of rape within their communities. They found that women engage in two basic types of precautionary behavior in response to their fear: isolating themselves, often indoors at home, in an attempt to protect themselves from harm; and behaving in a wary, street-wise fashion in the presence of danger. They also found that nearly all women restrict their own behavior, markedly reducing their freedom of movement, in response to perceived threats in the environment (Gordon and Riger, 1989).

With support from the National Institute of Justice (NIJ), Wesley Skogan embarked on a series of studies to learn more about preventive strategies against violent crime. One such project focused on victims of robberies, assaults, and rapes. It concluded that in a violent confrontation between strangers, victims who resist a rapist or robber could significantly reduce the risk that the crime will be completed, whether or not the attacker is armed (Block and Skogan, 1987).

As part of NIJ's "fear reduction" experiment launched in 1983, Skogan and Paul Lavrakas, analyzed a series of experimental strategies aimed at reducing citizens' fear of crime. Working with the Police Foundation and the police departments of Houston, Texas, and Newark, New Jersey, they found that increased police contact with citizens, over and above their law enforcement activities, could help reduce the fear of crime that pervades so many urban areas. In Houston, for example, opening a neighborhood police station or contacting citizens about problems not only helps reduce fear but also reduces the actual level of victimization.

Many of IPR's crime projects were based on studies conducted in Chicago. After a local television news exposé charged that Chicago police were systematically lowering the number of crimes reported to the Federal Bureau of Investigation, the Chicago Police Department conducted an internal audit in early 1983 to see whether its officers were indeed "killing crime" through faulty record keeping. The Illinois Department of Law Enforcement asked sociologist Andrew Gordon and political scientist Skogan to assess the audit's fairness. They recommended an ongoing review of crime-recording practices by the Chicago Police Department to ensure continued adherence to fair procedures (Skogan and Gordon, 1983). Subsequently, the department instituted an audit procedure that incorporated features similar to many of those suggested by the two scholars.

A few years later, IPR conducted a two-year evaluation for the Ford Foundation that cast serious doubts about the efficacy of neighborhood block watch programs in local crime prevention. It found that the efforts of five Chicago community groups to create and maintain block watches, with external funding but no substantial help from law enforcement, not only failed to reduce crime and fear or to improve neighborhood cohesiveness in any significant way, but in some cases may have produced the opposite effects.

The nation's most ambitious experiment in community policing is the subject of the largest criminal justice evaluation ever undertaken by IPR. Now in its seventh year, a research team directed by Wesley Skogan continues to monitor the process and effects of implementing Chicago's Alternative Policing Strategy and regularly shares its findings with the police and the community. The initiative has created turf-oriented teams of police officers with long-term beat assignments, extensively involved and empowered communities, and integrated the program with improved city services. It supports local problem solving by police and residents as they identify neighborhood priorities, develop plans of action, and mobilize police, city, and community resources to carry them out. Skogan's research team, comprising researchers from Northwestern, Loyola, and De Paul universities and the University of Illinois at Chicago, has issued five annual reports, twenty-three working papers, and two books so far on its findings (see Skogan and others, 1999).

Taken as a whole, these projects have helped shape the ways policymakers now think about crime. The impact of crime on victims and on the communities in which they live has been added to the traditional focus on offenders and their activities. IPR research has also raised awareness of the efforts of communities to secure their own safety rather than to depend solely on the police. Finally, IPR's twenty years of research on community policing has clarified the implementation problems big-city departments face and documented how properly implemented programs can reduce crime and fear.

Community Development. Foundation support enabled John McKnight, IPR's director of community studies, to develop and test a theory of community development that has altered traditional thinking about poor neighborhoods and energized a virtual revolution in neighborhood revitalization techniques. After three decades of research on low-income urban neighborhoods throughout the United States and Canada, McKnight became convinced that local communities are replete with assets—rather than needs—that can be tapped for revitalization and growth. His research team has collected data from over three hundred neighborhoods in twenty cities on the community development potential of such local assets as residents, local associations, schools, hospitals, churches, parks, and libraries.

McKnight's numerous projects have looked at nonmedical determinants of community health, providing basic necessities like food, water, and shelter with low-tech tools; empowering citizens by affording them access to city-held information on housing, public works projects, and crime; integrating developmentally disabled citizens into their communities; and developing new tools to redevelop older urban neighborhoods from within. In so doing, he has helped to redefine the giving philosophies of entities such as the United Way and foundations such as Kellogg, Winthrop Rockefeller, and Annie E. Casey.

His work led to the creation of IPR's Asset-Based Community Development Institute, whose mission is to assist local communities that are moving from the traditional needs and deficiencies approach to one that draws on their internal strengths. The stage was set for this work in the early 1970s when McKnight's ties to local community organizations prompted a study of redlining in Chicago, directed by sociologist Andrew Gordon. This research demonstrated the process by which federal policy and financial institutions were combining to deny low-income neighborhoods access to standard-rate mortgage funds. Subsequently community groups throughout the country used the findings to effect changes in state legislation and passage of the Community Reinvestment Act and the Home Mortgage Disclosure Act, which banned such discriminatory practices (Metzger and Weiss, 1988).

McKnight subsequently partnered with several community groups to identify the individual, associational, and financial resources available for use in local neighborhood revitalization efforts. The resulting "Capacity Inventory" has developed into a tool that is being used throughout the world to discover local assets within communities.

McKnight's group conducted a series of Chicago Innovations Forums from 1987 to 1992 that brought together research scholars and influential Chicagoans from diverse backgrounds to discuss some of the city's most pressing problems and to develop new initiatives for resolving them. Among the issues they tackled were community participation in decision making about local capital expenditures, Chicago public school reform, an afford- able housing agenda, community gardening, and community policing.

McKnight's work became formalized in 1995 as the Asset-Based Com- munity Development Institute. It is currently focusing research on the key role of associations in community building and how they can be mobilized to rebuild civil society in local communities, rejuvenate local economies, and strengthen public and private investments in community.

Looking Ahead

From its early mission to study and ameliorate pressing problems of urban life in Chicago, IPR has evolved into a public policy institute devoted to social issues of national scope. In the areas of poverty and social welfare, for example, IPR researchers in the 1980s focused on understanding the effects of the so-called Reagan Revolution on economic hardship in Chicago. This Chicago-as-laboratory approach led IPR researchers to contribute to a national debate on poverty and the measurement of material well-being. In the mid-1990s, the U.S. Department of Health and Human Services funded the Joint Center for Poverty Research, which has a national-level mission to conduct research and to advise the department on the effectiveness of pol- icies designed to reduce poverty, including the effects of welfare reforms.

In the area of inequality and race, IPR began with a faculty evaluation of the local Gautreaux program's relocation of families in public housing and went on to inspire the U.S. Department of Housing and Urban Development's National Moving to Opportunities program. Similarly, research on crime first focused on local Chicago communities and was funded by local foundations and organizations, but the federal government soon showed an interest in IPR's criminal justice research and provided federal funding. Finally, IPR research in community development began locally and spread nationally and internationally. IPR's many resource books and workbooks on asset-based community development currently guide hundreds of local government pol-icymakers, foundations, community groups, and social service agencies in the United States and abroad.

IPR faculty remain well positioned and committed to apply their inter-disciplinary research capabilities to many of the nation's most difficult and unsolved issues:

- Reforming the elementary and secondary educational system
- Implementing welfare reform in a way that strengthens families and pro-motes positive child development
- Increasing citizen participation in communities
- Defining the appropriate roles of federal, state, and local governments
- Understanding the causes of increasing income disparity between classes and races and developing policies to offset those differences
- Involving communities in innovative responses to combat crime
- Understanding the impact of the nation's racial and ethnic diversity and the effects of its growing elderly population

Since 1968, the diverse range of research topics has fluctuated accord-ing to changing times, and a single chapter can only suggest the breadth and depth of IPR's research. But what has remained constant throughout is the institute's emphasis on social problems and on social capacities to solve them.

References

Block, R., and Skogan, W. G. "Resistance and Nonfatal Outcomes in Stranger-to-Stranger Predatory Crime." *Violence and Victims,* 1987, *1,* 241–254.
Cook, F. L., and others. *Stability and Change in Economic Hardship: Chicago: 1983–1985.* Evanston, Ill.: Center for Urban Affairs and Policy Research, 1986.
Duncan, G. J., and others. *New Hope for People with Low Incomes: Two-Year Results of a Program to Reduce Poverty and Reform Welfare.* New York: Manpower Demonstration Research Project, 1999.
Gordon, M. T., and Riger, S. *The Female Fear.* New York: Free Press, 1989.
Hills v. Gautreaux, 425 U.S. 284 (1976).
Jencks, C. *Rethinking Social Policy: Race, Poverty, and the Underclass.* Cambridge, Mass.: Harvard University Press, 1992.
Jencks, C., and Peterson, P. E. (eds.). *The Urban Underclass.* Washington, D.C.: Brook-ings Institution, 1991.
Lewis, D. A. (ed.). *Reactions to Crime.* Thousand Oaks, Calif.: Sage, 1981.
Lewis, D. A., Riger, S., Rosenberg, H., and Wagenaar, H. *Worlds of the Mentally Ill: How Dein-stitutionalization Works in the City.* Carbondale: Southern Illinois University Press, 1991.
Lewis, D. A., and others. *State Hospital Utilization in Chicago: People, Problems, and Pol-icy.* Evanston, Ill.: Center for Urban Affairs and Policy Research, 1987.
Metzger, J. T., and Weiss, M., *The Role of Private Lending in Neighborhood Development: The Chicago Experience.* Evanston, Ill.: Center for Urban Affairs and Policy Research, 1988.
Skogan, W. G., and Gordon, A. C. "A Review of Detective Division Reporting Practices: A Report of the Chicago Police Department's Crime Classification Audit." In *Crime in Illinois.* Springfield: Illinois Department of Law Enforcement, 1983.
Skogan, W. G., and others. *On the Beat: Police and Community Problem Solving.* Boulder, Colo.: Westview Press, 1999.

Stockman, D. A. *The Triumph of Politics: How the Reagan Revolution Failed.* New York: HarperCollins, 1986.
Wilson, W. J. *The Truly Disadvantaged: The Inner City, the Underclass, and Public Policy.* Chicago: University of Chicago Press, 1987.

For Further Reading

Bradford, C. P., Grothaus, D. E., and Rubinowitz, L. S. *The Role of Mortgage Lending Practices in Older Urban Neighborhoods: Institutional Lenders, Regulatory Agencies, and Their Community Impacts.* Evanston, Ill.: Center for Urban Affairs and Policy Research, 1975.
Center for Urban Affairs and Policy Research. *Center for Urban Affairs: The First Decade 1968–1978.* Evanston, Ill.: Center for Urban Affairs and Policy Research, 1978.
Conquergood, D., Friesema, P., Hunter, A., and Mansbridge, J. *Dispersed Ethnicity and Community Integration: Newcomers and Established Residents in the Albany Park Area of Chicago.* Evanston, Ill.: Center for Urban Affairs and Policy Research, 1990.
Cook, F. L., and Barrett, E. J. *Support for the American Welfare State: The Views of Congress and the Public.* New York: Columbia University Press, 1992.
Ford Foundation. *The Common Good, Social Welfare, and the American Future.* New York: Ford Foundation, 1989.
Manikas, P. M., Heinz, J. P., Trossman, M. S., and Doppelt, J. C. *Criminal Justice Policymaking: Boundaries and Borderlands.* Evanston, Ill.: Center for Urban Affairs and Policy Research, 1990.
McKnight, J. L., and Kretzmann, J. P. *Building Communities from the Inside Out: A Path Toward Finding and Mobilizing a Community's Assets.* Evanston, Ill.: Center for Urban Affairs and Policy Research, 1993.
Northwestern University. "New Center for Urban Affairs Created at Northwestern University." Press release, Oct. 17, 1968.
Pate, A. M., Wycoff, M. A., Skogan, W. G., and Sherman, L. W. *Reducing Fear of Crime in Houston and Newark.* Washington, D.C.: National Institute of Justice/Police Foundation, 1986.
Rosenbaum, D. P., Lewis, D. A., and Grant, J. A. *The Impact of Community Crime Prevention Programs in Chicago: Can Neighborhood Organizations Make a Difference?* Evanston, Ill.: Center for Urban Affairs and Policy Research, 1985.
Rosenbaum, J. E., and Popkin, S. J. *Economic and Social Impacts of Housing Integration.* Evanston, Ill.: Center for Urban Affairs and Policy Research, 1990.
Rosenbaum, J. E., Rubinowitz, L. S., and Kulieke, M. J. *Low-Income Black Children in White Suburban Schools.* Evanston, Ill.: Center for Urban Affairs and Policy Research, 1986.
Rubinowitz, L. S., and Rosenbaum, J. E. *Crossing the Class and Color Lines: From Public Housing to White Suburbia.* Chicago: University of Chicago Press, 2000.
Skogan, W. G., and Hartnett, S. M. *Community Policing, Chicago Style.* New York: Oxford University Press, 1997.
Weiss, C. H. "Ideology, Interests, and Information: The Basis for Policy Positions." In D. Callahan and B. Jennings (eds). *Ethics, the Social Sciences, and Policy Analysis.* New York: Plenum, 1983.

FAY LOMAX COOK is director of the Institute for Policy Research at Northwestern University and professor of human development and social policy in the School of Education and Social Policy.

AUDREY CHAMBERS is director of publications for the Institute for Policy Research.

6

The McCormack Institute has been a leader in independent and objective assessment of highly charged local issues.

The McCormack Institute

Robert L. Woodbury

The John W. McCormack Institute of Public Affairs at the University of Massachusetts at Boston, named for the man who served as Speaker of the U.S. House of Representatives from 1962 to 1971, developed from an unusual set of circumstances. In higher education, Massachusetts, and certainly greater Boston, has been uniquely dominated by distinguished private colleges and universities. The most eminent of these institutions, however, have had little or sporadic interest in politics or public policy issues at the state and local levels.

Origins

The creation of the Boston campus of the University of Massachusetts in the Dorchester section of Boston in 1974 marked the kind of public commitment, concern, and mission that would become embodied in the establishment of the McCormack Institute. From its inception, the institute focused primarily on issues of local, state, and regional concern in Massachusetts and New England; to fuse applied policy research, education, and public service in a single mission; and to carry out its activities through conferences, general education endeavors on and off campus, publications, and extensive outreach. Its staff would embody serious scholarly capacities with a love of politics and public policy.

McCormack also sought to bring under the umbrella of the institute the Boston Urban Observatory, which had conducted contracted studies for the City of Boston on subjects from fair housing to tax policy; the Center for Survey Research, which had done many funded studies for both public and private clients; and the Policy Studies Center, which had sponsored many successful policy and political conferences and various studies on the

Massachusetts fiscal system. Numerous faculties had also been active in applied policy research regarding Boston and Massachusetts and would bring their activities and expertise to the institute.

The McCormack Institute began with powerful patrons and entrepreneurial leadership. In fact, the entrepreneurial leader was critical to the participation of the powerful patrons. Edmund Beard, a young professor of political science at UMass with a passionate interest in American government, would be the key figure in the institute's initiation and development. He loved the messy world of Massachusetts politics, was an excellent lecturer, and had an indefatigable capacity for academic entrepreneurship. Beard's effort in establishing the McCormack Institute is a case study in legislative and bureaucratic politics. His ability to leverage key figures in Congress, the state legislature, and the university administration was critical.

Building on an internship that Beard had established as a young professor for a UMass student in the Speaker's Office of the U.S. House of Representatives, he developed links with the key staff and Congressman Tip O'Neill. When Beard discovered in 1983 that Congress had authorized a line item expenditure of $2 million to establish a center at the University of Oklahoma in honor of former Speaker Carl Albert, he moved to propose a similar tribute to former Speaker John W. McCormack. O'Neill quickly agreed, and a $3 million endowment was proposed through Tip O'Neill's good friend, fellow congressman, and successor in McCormack's district, Joseph Moakley. In 1991, Moakley followed up with another $3 million appropriation for endowment that would allow the institute to broaden its portfolio to include an international dimension.

As he worked on his academic and congressional strategy, Beard also turned to his longtime friend, state senator Chester Atkins, who in 1983 was the chairman of the Massachusetts Senate Ways and Means Committee. Atkins cleared a proposed $250,000 state appropriation with the Speaker of the Senate and later president of the University of Massachusetts, William Bulger. In 1983, the McCormack Institute of Public Affairs was officially launched only a few minutes from the State House on the urban campus of the state's public university.

A special combination of unusual circumstances had launched the McCormack Institute in a notable and auspicious way: a vacuum in academic participation in local civic affairs, special interest by key state legislators, a track record of several projects already present on the Boston campus, commitment to the idea and the mission it embodied from the highest levels on campus, a significant endowment at a university that had no other endowment, and, most critically, the entrepreneurial leadership of a young political science professor.

Organization and Operation

The organization of the institute, its mode of operation, and the variety of its programmatic activities differed from typical academic departments. These differences reflected the realities associated with trying to bridge the gap between the world of politics and the world of academia. University expertise resided in a community that valued the search for truth, the ideal of objective inquiry, the respect for theory, and the more leisurely pace of scholarship; these values did not mesh easily with the world of electoral politics, compromise, an omnipresent media, and the urgencies of legislation and government operations.

From the beginning, the institute addressed this challenge in several ways:

The core full-time staff was kept small, never more than ten to fifteen people, in order to maintain maximum flexibility in attracting and recruiting expertise.

The professional staff mixed faculty who had regular academic appointments and relevant policy interests with experienced and thoughtful practitioners, sometimes retired, usually from Massachusetts government, politics, and public affairs.

The institute took advantage of mixed funding streams—endowment income, the state budget line, university resources, and grant money from governments and foundations—to provide flexibility and some independence. McCormack collaborated with other agencies or organizations on and off campus to maximize value and impact.

The institute infused a teaching and educational mission into its everyday life, which, given the fact that most students lived in the working world, encouraged a fusion of the academic and the practical.

The institute consciously and astutely exploited all avenues for public visibility.

The issues that the McCormack Institute addressed over the years ranged widely but grew out of the particular mission that came with the founding: focus on issues critical to the geographical region, some growing attention to emerging democracies as encouraged by Congressman Moakley, and UMass Boston's special responsibility to address the needs of poor and underserved populations in the metropolitan area. A few examples suggest the variety of undertakings:

- Assisting the city of Chelsea when the courts placed it in receivership
- Working with the state to maximize Medicaid reimbursements from the federal government
- Addressing the challenge of metropolitan regionalism
- Proposing alternatives to make pay levels in the courts more equitable
- Evaluating the impact of welfare reform in cases of domestic violence
- Polling on subjects from gubernatorial races to the quality of community life
- Examining the rule of law in China
- Addressing the vagaries of the Northern Ireland peace process

In the mid-1990s, the institute organized its activities into four centers that reflected both the nature and origin of those activities. The Center for

State and Local Policy tended to focus on fiscal, operational, and political issues of state and local government and also oversaw the McCormack Poll, an in-house survey of voters on key public issues. The Center for Social Policy, which also addressed issues in Massachusetts, concentrated on topics such as homelessness, family policy, welfare reform, and themes that linked to underserved populations. The Center for Women in Politics and Public Policy served a networking and educational role in Massachusetts and conducted studies that related to the status of women and issues that most concerned women. The Center for Democracy and Development addressed the international piece of the McCormack's mission by focusing on issues of democratization in places like Eastern Europe, sub-Saharan Africa, China, and elsewhere. Padraig O'Malley, a prominent fellow from the founding, was a major scholar and activist in both the peace process in Northern Ireland and the transition from apartheid in South Africa. Many projects, if not most, at McCormack, however, cut across center-lines; projects abroad almost always drew on expertise that was nominally housed in another center at the institute, as well as other institutes at UMass Boston.

The fundamental question for the McCormack Institute and UMass Boston, however, did not relate to the range of studies and projects it undertook, but the role and effectiveness it achieved in improving and enhancing government and governance. The answer is complex and elusive. The results of the study by the Center for Social Policy of the relationship between welfare reform and domestic violence directly and immediately changed Massachusetts's welfare regulations two days before it was even officially released in 1997. The astonishing role that O'Malley played in convening the entire range of political leadership of Northern Ireland with Nelson Mandela and his colleagues in the Western Cape of South Africa in 1997 was followed directly by the talks that led to the Good Friday agreement a year later. The massive effort by the ANCHoR project (officially the Automated National Client-Specific Homeless Services Recording System) over several years to build a state system for tracking the homeless in Boston and Massachusetts as a whole promises to be a model of modernizing state government to enhance social delivery systems. The AIDS issue of the *New England Journal of Public Policy* in 1988, subsequently published as a book, was a singular leadership effort in developing a broader public and political consciousness of the dimensions of the problem. The series of studies that culminated in a comparative examination of how each of the six New England states dealt with the state budget collapses of the late 1980s provoked considerable discussion of alternative ways to provide better state fiscal management. The efforts of the Center for Women in Politics and Public Policy to bring hundreds of women into more public and political activities in Massachusetts over a decade has already been reflected in a greater presence of program participants in civic life.

Making an Impact

The alchemy of public and political policy formulation, decision making, and implementation is murky at best. A deeper and more analytical examination of the ways in which the McCormack Institute has endeavored to make an impact on these processes may provide a more compelling assessment. Several modes of endeavor have marked the McCormack enterprise.

Serving as an Independent Analyzer. In 1997, the institute was commissioned by the state legislature to examine the mounting costs of the nation's largest public works project, the so-called Big Dig. Funded primarily by the National Transportation Act, the Central Artery/Tunnel project was designed to replace all the major highways over and through Boston with an underground tunnel system that would also provide twenty-seven acres of open land in the heart of the city. Not only was the project one of the most ambitious urban infrastructure undertakings in history, but the entire $10.8 billion effort was intended to be completed over twenty years with no removal of housing or businesses, no interruption of everyday life and commercial activity, and with enhancement to the environment of the city. The national press, most vividly in a devastating *60 Minutes* report, and local observers, most persistently in reports from the state auditor, portrayed the entire project as the worst example of pork, boondoggle, and mismanagement.

The chairman of the Massachusetts Senate Ways and Means Committee sought on behalf of the legislature in 1996 some independent assessment of whether financial savings were possible, particularly as the burden of the project would increasingly fall on Massachusetts taxpayers. Given the long history of debates and controversy around the Big Dig and the widespread involvement of politicians, government employees, and innumerable interest groups, there were very few candidates for an independent evaluation of what was going on. The McCormack Institute received a $325,000 grant from state government to analyze the reasons for the steadily increasing estimated costs of the project and to explore any alternatives that might lessen or control costs.

The seventy-four-page highly analytical study, prepared by an interdisciplinary team headed by a just retired international vice president of the Arthur D. Little Company, essentially concluded that once the political decision had been made to undertake the massive venture and the political commitment had been made not to disrupt the quality of life of the city, the actual management of the project seemed to be carried out in a professional and fiscally responsible fashion. For the first time, readers could understand that the cause of the $10.8 billion price tag was not waste, corruption, and mismanagement but three almost equal components: the actual engineering and physical cost of construction, the substantial mitigation costs of ensuring that the city could continue normal operations with an enhanced environment, and the consequences of inflation over a decades-long period of planning, delay, and actual building. The report did warn that publicly reported estimates of the costs seemed low and that careful controls, good management, and luck would be required to keep the financial outlay within bounds.

The study, titled "Managing the Central Artery/Tunnel Project: An Exploration of Potential Cost Savings" (Sloan, 1997), received front-page coverage from the *Boston Globe*, periodic citation from policymakers for its authoritative analysis, and occasional swipes from political leaders with one agenda or another. Hundreds of interested parties sought copies of the report. And shortly after it appeared, it disappeared from public view. The several recommendations for legislative action (such as reducing the costs of police surveillance) resulted in no immediate action, but several suggestions for management redirection were pursued because in most cases, they gave political cover for steps that management already wanted to implement.

Education and Training of Public Servants at the State and Local Levels. From the beginning, McCormack has housed the master's program in public affairs (MSPA), and a senior fellow at McCormack has, under the oversight of the provost or graduate dean, directed the program. The program has always reflected the style and mission of McCormack rather than a particular academic department. Each year between twenty and twenty-five working adults are admitted in a single cohort for a two-year proscribed year-round program that meets for two nights a week and periodic weekends. Most students are state employees, from both the legislative and executive branches, with a sprinkling of state legislators, other public sector employees, newspaper people, and various others from the private sector with civic interests. Most are from Massachusetts, and most are in their thirties or forties. As with the institute itself, the faculty come from academic departments and the public sector. The curriculum embodies policy analysis and organizational and management studies, with subjects focused on the economics and politics of Massachusetts and New England.

With over three hundred graduates, most of whom have remained in the public sector in Massachusetts, the MSPA program may well be the institute's most enduring contribution to state and regional governance. The network of alumni also gives McCormack a particular access and leverage in government affairs. When the institute undertook the Big Dig study in 1996, for example, the chief staff person to the director of the Big Dig was an MSPA alumna, and the chief staff person to the House Transportation Committee was a current MSPA student.

The institute provides financial support and project opportunities for significant numbers of students in the full-time doctoral program in public policy and graduate students in other relevant departments. At any given time, six or more funded projects at McCormack may employ graduate students. The Big Dig study, for example, provided two doctoral students with full support for a year. Undergraduates interested in public affairs are attracted to McCormack because they enjoy the excitement and involvement of its activities.

Publishing on Major Public Policy Issues. McCormack encourages broader examination of various public policy issues through serious publications: so-called Occasional Papers, books authored by senior staff, and special reports.

The institute's *New England Journal of Public Policy* is the most ambitious continuing effort to put forth serious inquiry into major public policy issues important to the region. Published twice a year, the *New England Journal* devotes one issue to a particular subject (for example, the reorganization of mental health services in the commonwealth) and one to a single theme (such as homelessness, the AIDS crisis, or the emergence of the Latino community in New England). Several theme issues have also been published as books by independent presses to capture a larger market.

Convener and Catalyst on Important Public Issues. From its inception, the McCormack Institute assumed leadership for public forums and conferences that brought together scholars, practitioners, political leaders, and other interested parties to explore critical issues. The subjects might range from a more general exploration of the role of women in public life in New England to a legislative briefing on family policy legislation.

The McCormack's convening role on the theme of regionalism is illustrative of a continuing leadership role as a convener and catalyst. In an area of the country where the local town meeting is sacrosanct, the McCormack sought to stimulate a dialogue around the realities and possibilities associated with regional solutions. Senior fellow Robert C. Wood (1997), former secretary of the U.S. Department of Housing and Urban Development, wrote an occasional paper on the history and prospects of metropolitan regionalism in greater Boston; senior fellow Barry Bluestone led a team of scholars who made a major Ford-funded study of greater Boston in transition (Bluestone and Stevenson, 2000); and the director of the institute served on the governor's commission on Boston area regionalism chaired by the mayor of Boston. These efforts were entwined with an annual conference on the subject of regionalism in greater Boston.

In addition, the McCormack Institute took leadership with the New England Board of Higher Education (NEHBE) in exploring the prospects of regional solutions to New England–wide challenges. Many issues, from transportation to conservation to economic development, clearly crossed the lines of all six New England states and seemed amenable to some collaborative efforts in public policy. One concrete result was the creation, under NEHBE's umbrella, of the New England Public Policy Collaborative, which began to inventory and gather together the applied research capacities of more than two hundred diverse centers and institutes across the region. Second, in preparation for a New England Conference of the Collaborative in 1999, NEHBE surveyed one thousand New England leaders on public issues facing the region, and the McCormack Poll conducted a parallel survey of a representative sample of New England households.

Permanent Mechanisms to Modernize State Government. On many occasions, the institute has been entrusted, in close collaboration with state agencies, to help develop a new operational capacity for state or local government. McCormack, for example, initiated and became the state's operational agency for the massive Medicaid reimbursement program over a period of many years. This effort brought savings of hundreds of millions of dollars to the state, as it did in other states across the country, richly rewarded McCormack with flexible funds, and became a regularized part of state operations.

A more recent example, still in development, is the effort to create a computerized data system for the tracking of the homeless, a burgeoning problem throughout the commonwealth. The ANCHoR project, as it is called, costs over $400,000 a year and requires sensitive attention to innumerable constituencies: local, state, and federal governments; hundreds of halfway houses and other intake centers; untold bureaucracies and political stakeholders; and thousands of homeless people. The project is an endeavor that may serve as a model elsewhere in the country.

Empowering New Civic Constituencies. In its early years, the McCormack Institute was a bastion of white males, not unlike policy centers elsewhere and certainly not unlike Massachusetts and Boston politics itself. Even today Massachusetts is particularly slow in bringing significant numbers of women and people of color into roles of political leadership. The McCormack Institute has begun to play a more significant part in improving governance by helping enable new constituencies to become part of civic life.

The McCormack became the home in 1992 of the Center for Women in Politics and Public Policy, once housed at Boston College, which has become the state's primary center of networking individuals, convening around relevant issues, and encouraging policy papers on issues of particular concern to women. The center's largest funded project at the end of the decade was a major study of the status of women and girls in Massachusetts that engaged communities, including women of color and across socioeconomic lines, in every corner of the state.

A more modest effort by the institute was the use of the McCormack Poll to enhance public visibility for interracial issues in the state. In the spring of 1998, the McCormack Poll not only surveyed the usual sample of five hundred citizens, but also added targeted samples of one hundred each in the African American, Latino, and Asian American communities. The results highlighted areas of difference and commonality on major issues among racial constituencies and also exploded some myths about attitudes and behavior.

Using the Popular Media. In its effort to help enhance civic dialogue on important issues of public policy, the McCormack Institute has always been, uncharacteristically for most academic institutions, particularly attentive to the popular media.

McCormack senior fellows, numbering from fifteen to twenty, are regularly part of the media scene in greater Boston and frequently at the national and international level. This critical part of McCormack's activities is fed by the regular studies and reports that are issued, often accompanied by press releases and sometimes by press conferences or interviews, and the McCormack Institute's *Media Directory* (1997), which portrays the expertise and experience of McCormack staff and affiliates. In addition, and more aggressively, McCormack people write op-ed pieces on a regular basis, moderate political debates, serve as commentators on local and national radio and television programs, and can be counted on by local reporters to be generally available for comment on fast-breaking stories.

Enhancing Governance on a Global Scale. Working on challenges of improved governance outside the United States became of increasing priority to the McCormack for three reasons. First, individual faculty members and staff took increasing interest in developments abroad, particularly following the collapse of the Soviet system, the resurgence of China and Asia in general, and the emergence of new nations across Africa. Second, the additional installment for the endowment that Congressman Moakley garnered for the institute acknowledged Moakley's interest in emerging democracies in poorer regions of the world. Third, and unanticipated when the institute was founded, was that the "devolution" movement away from centralized government would become a global phenomenon sweeping the developing world. Suddenly what the institute knew the most about—the intricacies of local and state government from issues of representative government, taxation, or water quality at the local level—was just what civic leaders in sub-Saharan Africa and elsewhere were particularly interested in. Almost overnight issues of national and international policy—and institutes or centers that focused on them—were of lesser priority to thousands of citizen leaders who were wrestling with local challenges of governance and democratization.

This reality led McCormack into a variety of projects, usually funded by the federal government, that took the institute abroad and brought foreign nationals to McCormack. A delegation of justices from China came to McCormack to explore various aspects of the criminal justice system in the commonwealth; the workshop included participation in court trials and interviews with inmates in prisons. A delegation from McCormack spent several weeks in Mali, Senegal, and the Cameroon, working with counterpart Africans on issues such as the control of waste and fraud, local taxation systems, auditing methodologies, and affirmative action efforts.

Continuing and Future Challenges

Several dilemmas continue to challenge the conduct of a university-based public policy institute at UMass Boston. In the effort to be both useful and thoughtful, to honor both the messy world of politics and governance and the quite different values of an academic community, the institute has persistently struggled with several issues.

Neutrality and Objectivity. How does the institute address the aspiration to neutrality and objectivity in an enterprise laced with partisanship and advocacy? There has been no satisfactory answer, particularly when the McCormack has naturally attracted people who care deeply about public issues, work at a university with a commitment to underserved populations, and tend to be political activists. In addition, academics at UMass interested in issues such as homelessness or family violence, for example, have strong personal commitments. The tentative, even uncertain accommodation seems to be to continue to insist on the careful use of evidence and the consideration of the various dimensions of complex questions by all staff; recognize that any particular study will engage scholars who have strong values and commitments, but ensure that the institute as a whole accommodates a wide spectrum of views; and protect dearly the university's presumption of offering neutral ground for disparate parties in the search for the good and the true. This is easier said than done. But well-balanced advisory committees or review sessions, for both the institute and its centers and to individual projects, can ensure other perspectives.

Applied Research. The commitment of McCormack to undertake useful applied research at the state and local levels invited some difficult choices. State legislators and state bureaucrats often sought inexpensive alternatives to research staff of their own and also looked for studies or evaluations that reinforced some preconceived position. There is a difference, if often hazy, between the McCormack's contract to study the fiscal dimensions of the Big Dig and the temptation to aid Democratic members of the Transportation Committees of the House and Senate in writing legislation on construction policy that they sought to enact. Similarly, serving as the intellectual think tank for the development of Medicaid reimbursement schemes for the state, as McCormack did for several years, soon became a quasi-governmental operation itself. Eventually the institute abandoned the function.

Enlisting Faculty. The McCormack has faced the continuing problem of enlisting competent and able faculty who are interested in state policy issues, can meet the timetables and necessities of governmental actors, and feel rewarded in the academic context. McCormack's efforts in housing policy are illustrative. The major work on the ANCHoR project to set up a model tracking system is staffed almost wholly by nonprofessorial employees; several studies of housing policy, on the other hand, have been led by a mix of university faculty and senior staff professionals. In the Big Dig study, no full-time university faculty member played any role. Commissioning faculty on a reduced load during the year and for the summer has brought many successes, but mismatches and disappointments as well.

Identifying Niches. A challenge has been to identify the best policy niches where expertise could be aggregated, demand existed, and comparative advantage might lie. To say that McCormack emphasized Massachusetts, Boston, and New England policy concerns does not reduce the agenda of priorities very much. Part of the answer was simply opportunism: the institute was asked to do the Big Dig study, which was well funded, important to the state and legislature, and highly visible.

Over time, however, several niches became well established: links to underserved communities, state fiscal policy and practice, community and family violence, housing policy, some aspects of welfare reform and family policy in general, issues of concern to women, higher education itself, statewide polling and the use of survey research, regionalism in both greater Boston and New England, and problems of democratization and local governance abroad. But the mix of choices was less a product of careful planning than a combination of a well-understood mission, an opportunity, a sense of the strengths and weaknesses of UMass Boston and McCormack, and individual entrepreneurship that the institute fostered for the campus and the region.

The Media. A continuing challenge relates to the indispensable reality of the media. In Boston this means the omnipresent *Boston Globe* and its legion of reporters and commentators focusing on issues of state and local politics and government. Other media—the *Boston Herald,* radio, and television—are important, but if the *Globe* does not report it, then it has no standing. For major studies, the *Globe* was often quite clear: "If we get it first, it gets on the front page." The McCormack Institute had no consistent answer to this "deal" and bumbled from episode to episode. In the case of the Big Dig study, for example, the *Globe* got it first, ran a front-page story bringing attention to the report, distorted the analysis with a misleading headline, and antagonized several politicians who thought they should have had the report before the *Globe* did.

In addition, because Boston is the center of most political activity in the region (or thinks that it is), McCormack staff developed major relationships and instant availability with a number of newspaper, radio, and television outlets. Someone from the media who wanted a response, often very quotable, to almost any breaking story called McCormack. Institute staff often provided opinion pieces on the editorial pages and on talk shows. In short, the institute has been a media player on a wide range of issues. How this capacity can be used to contribute best to a more informed public and to better governance is a continuing challenge.

Conclusion

The McCormack Institute's directions for the future will build on a rich past. Its role in graduate education will probably grow as UMass Boston gives greater priority to programs in public policy and management, as well as the mission of the only public university in the commonwealth's urban center. The established priority for attending to issues of state and local government and politics can only increase in an era of devolution. Some more recent niches, such as the role of women in public life, housing policy, and opportunities in sub-Saharan Africa, seem likely to expand.

Several challenges faced by state and local government in Massachusetts will probably become of increasing importance to McCormack as well: coping with and incorporating new technologies, as McCormack is doing with ANCHoR; continuing to emphasize the potential for regional approaches, as McCormack has done in helping establish the New England Policy Collaborative; becoming much more attentive to global imperatives and opportunities, as the institute has begun with projects concerned with democratization and issue around the rule of law; and addressing issues of diversity and community empowerment, as in the case of the impact of the Center for Women in Politics and Public Policy and work with the three ethnic institutes at UMass Boston.

The McCormack Institute lives in a volatile and uneasy halfway house between politics and government, epitomized by civic life in Boston, and academic politics and culture, well represented in the University of Massachusetts. The tension, ambiguity, and uncertainty that a mission of academic service to the cause of better governance embodies has been right for McCormack in the past and will no doubt serve the commonwealth well in the future.

References

Bluestone, B., and Stevenson, M. H. *The Boston Renaissance: Race, Space, and Economic Change in an American Metropolis.* New York: Russell Sage Foundation, 2000.

McCormack Institute. *Media Directory, 1997–1998.* Boston: McCormack Institute, 1997.

Sloan, A. K. "Managing the Central Artery/Tunnel Project: An Exploration of Potential Cost Savings." Boston: McCormack Institute, 1997.

Wood, R. L. *Eastward Ho: Issues and Options in Regional Development for the Metropolitan Boston Region.* Boston: McCormack Institute, 1997.

For Further Reading

Abelda, R. *An Economic Profile of Women in Massachusetts.* Boston: McCormack Institute, 1995.

Dickert, J. *A Policy Brief: Making Family Leave More Affordable in Massachusetts.* Boston: McCormack Institute, 1999.

Friedman, D. H. *Over the Edge: Cuts and Changes in Housing, Income Support, and Homeless Programs in Massachusetts.* Boston: McCormack Institute, 1977.

Hardy-Fanta, C., Waantanabe, P., and Di Natale, L. *Conflict and Convergence: Race, Public Opinion, and Political Behavior in Massachusetts.* Boston: McCormack Institute, 1998.

Manley, R. (ed.). *The Issues Book: Public Policy Issues in Massachusetts.* Boston: McCormack Institute, 2000.

ROBERT L. WOODBURY *is former director of the John W. McCormack Institute of Public Affairs at the University of Massachusetts at Boston and former chancellor of the University of Maine System.*

7

*The Rockefeller Institute convenes a wide variety of
partners to address issues of governmental capacity,
reform, and implementation.*

The Nelson A. Rockefeller Institute of Government: From State to National Focus on Political and Policy Studies

Thomas Gais, Catherine Lawrence

The Nelson A. Rockefeller Institute of Government, the public policy research institute of the State University of New York (SUNY), was founded in 1981. SUNY trustees established the institute to build and facilitate relationships between the sixty-four-campus state university system and the state government. However, the institute has moved away from this early position and emerged as a more autonomous organization with a permanent staff, its own research agenda, an independent base of funding, a national network of scholars who contribute to its work, and a nationwide audience of government officials, academicians, policy experts, and citizens interested in the changing roles and challenges of state and local governments.

For much of its early history, the Rockefeller Institute was viewed as an integral part of SUNY, and especially the University at Albany (SUNY-Albany). It was created in conjunction with the Nelson A. Rockefeller College of Public Affairs and Policy, the graduate school of public affairs that includes the university departments of public administration and political science and its schools of social welfare, information sciences, and criminal justice. SUNY chancellor Clifton Wharton requested proposals for a state university tribute to Nelson A. Rockefeller, governor of New York State from 1958 to 1973; and Warren Ilchman, vice president for research at SUNY-Albany, proposed bringing together university faculty involved in the applied social sciences. Partly because of the university's location in the state capital and partly because of its large investment in public policy and public affairs under the presidency of Vince O'Leary (1978–1989), applied social research was a strength of the

Albany campus. However, the faculty and departments involved in public affairs were dispersed throughout the campus. When the chancellor received two proposals for a tribute to Rockefeller, one to create a college of public affairs and the other to create a public policy research center, he joined the two ideas to create Rockefeller College and the Rockefeller Institute.

The early mission of the Rockefeller Institute was to help the state university "centrally as well as on its various campuses, respond to needs of discussion, instruction, and research on public issues of importance to New York State." It was expected to be a vehicle through which scholars and government officials across New York could share information, identify and address problems, and find ways of collaborating with one another. "Through fellowships, internships, conferences, and publications," the institute would "mobilize SUNY's vast range of instructional, research, and service resources" (Nelson A. Rockefeller Institute, 1999).

Although the institute was expected to draw on the expertise throughout the SUNY system, it had a special relationship from the beginning with SUNY-Albany. According to the institute's by-laws, the director of the institute, appointed by the SUNY board of trustees, would also serve as the provost of the Rockefeller College of Public Affairs and Policy. The by-laws also created a board of overseers whose duties include acting as an advisory to the chancellor regarding the programs, policies, procedures, and personnel of the institute.

The Early Years

The Rockefeller Institute began with a provost-director, an elegant building, and little else. As David Andersen recalls (interview with author, Dec. 15, 1999), Warren Ilchman, who was named to the provost-director position, "bought a set of dishes and started holding events. He just did things." He established a fellowship program, an annual competitive process in which applicants throughout the SUNY system proposed research projects to be pursued during a semester or academic year at the institute. Research from the projects was sometimes published by the institute, often in its Special Reports series. With the use of the fellows and institute volunteers—members of the Albany community or sometimes spouses of administrators and fellows—the institute began holding events.

The issues addressed in these events were broad in focus and varied in subject. Conceived as a neutral ground for the discussion of contentious ideas, the conferences typically included SUNY-wide faculty and state and local government officials. "There was a kind of an opportunistic quality to the early years," Andersen recalls. "We were always beating the bushes, always trying to invite everyone. A big statistic in the annual report to the overseers was how many public officials had visited the institute that year." Early activities at the institute were thus primarily focused on bringing government officials and faculty together. The specific topics addressed were important, but there was little continuity or sustained attention to particular issues as the subjects varied with the interests of the fellows who happened to be at the institute that year.

A look at early publications from the Rockefeller Institute reveals this diversity and emphasis on government-university collaboration. The publications spanned a broad spectrum of issues important to New York at the time, sometimes authored jointly by faculty and state agency staff from all over the state. Issues ranged from shellfish sanitation agreements, to learning disabilities, to Indian land claims. Authors hailed from many of the state universities, private universities, and government agencies.

The institute emphasized interpersonal relations as it tried to build greater trust between academics and policymakers—and between divided policymakers. One early participant likened the mission of the institute to the traditions of the Iroquois, native peoples of New York State. The six Iroquois nations practiced intense individualism, but when a conflict occurred or important decisions arose, representatives of each nation gathered at council meetings. During the meetings, they tried to reconcile differences, but if they disagreed, they honored these differences (E. Brunger, personal communication, Feb. 4, 2000). Similarly, when diverse groups gathered at the Rockefeller Institute, everyone laid down their stripes and conversed in peace, no matter their affiliation.

Norman Hurd was especially important in emphasizing and smoothing these relationships. As the longest director of the New York State Division of Budget (1982–1985), Hurd served two governors and was known as a gentleman with great personal integrity and many contacts. Upon his retirement as budget director, Hurd took on the institute as a personal project, dedicating many years to developing a support network around it. He gathered an impressive cadre of senior public officials, many of whom served on steering committees of the institute's board of overseers. This group laid a foundation of trust as well as encouraged the involvement of state and local government officials in the events at the institute.

One example of these early activities was the New York State Project 2000, which produced a report in 1986 (Nelson A. Rockefeller Institute, 1986). Project 2000 was a collaborative effort by state government, the private sector, and the university to pool resources into a strategic planning initiative, to "give thoughtful consideration to critical issues that will affect New York throughout the balance of the century" (p. iii). Advisory panels of twenty or so experts were convened at the institute around economic development, corrections and criminal justice, water resources, population, housing, electricity, economic structure, long-term care, and science and technology. Each panel worked with the Rockefeller Institute to prepare a report and conference for its release. Governor Mario Cuomo endorsed the reports in the form of an introductory letter, praising their contents as well as the processes that produced them for closing the gap between state government and the academic community.

In 1987, Warren Ilchman left the institute to become vice president for academic affairs at SUNY-Albany, and David Andersen, dean of the Rockefeller College Graduate School of Public Affairs, was named interim director. The institute had grown quickly, but financing remained a continuing issue. In its early years, the Research Foundation of the State University of New York provided the institute's core operating support. As the institute took on more ambitious projects, however, it repeatedly overspent its operating budget. Under Andersen's leadership, the institute began to expand its grant and contract research activities. In addition, Andersen asked the New York State legislature to increase the budget. It was given a modest state appropriation to cover a portion of its annual operating costs. The annual New York State budget provided this funding to SUNY, which in turn allocated it to the institute.

Still, the budget was small and the institute's activities were quite limited. Other problems were also evident. With little research staff of its own, the institute relied on guest researchers from the SUNY system to provide expertise. Because the institute served largely as a means for outside scholars to pursue specific, short-term, research interests, it had little control over its own agenda, and public officials did not know whether they could turn to the institute for answers to any particular questions. The idea of creating an institution that facilitated interactions between New York's governments and its state university may have been an attractive one, but without a substantial budget and a greater staff capacity, the institute often seemed to be an empty vessel in search of something to give it meaning and character. There were no overall themes as it moved from one project to another, nor did it show a particular style of conducting research. Throughout the 1980s, the institute had developed no real institutional memory or cumulative aggregation of expertise.

A Shift Toward Greater Autonomy

In the 1990s, the Rockefeller Institute emerged as a more autonomous research center with a clearly developed expertise and substantive focus. The scope of its work expanded to include multistate and national concerns, it recruited its own staff and established a national network of collaborators, and it adopted its own distinctive analytical style. Although it still works directly with New York State government on a number of issues, the selection of those issues grows out of the institute's own research priorities: specifically, the structure and operation of state and local governments, the implementation and management of social policies, fiscal trends and patterns among state and local governments, public and higher education, and urban and neighborhood affairs. And although its overall dependence on SUNY faculty has declined, particularly in the last half of the 1990s, the institute still retains close relations with the scholars at SUNY-Albany.

Most of these developments occurred after Richard P. Nathan became director of the institute in the fall of 1989. Nathan established research groups with distinct themes soon after his arrival. He created the Center for the Study of the States to focus on fiscal changes at the state level, and he recruited the economist Steven Gold to direct it. The Center for Legislative Studies, headed by Michael Malbin of SUNY-Albany, was also established in 1990. Its research encompassed such issues as term limits for state legislators, campaign finance reform, and changes in executive-legislative relationships. In 1993, the Center for New York State and Local Government Affairs was created. Directed by Gerald Benjamin of SUNY-New Paltz, its work tended to focus on issues of state-local relationships, regionalization, and state constitutional change. Finally, under the directorship of Frank Thompson of SUNY-Albany and the chairmanship of former governor of Mississippi, William Winter, the Commission for the State and Local Public Service (referred to as the Winter Commission) was created to bring together the best information and increase public knowledge about the capacity of states for strong and effective executive leadership.

Rather than one institute-wide program, most research projects fell under the auspices of one of the research centers, and this structure helped direct the expanding work of the institute. At the same time, the research centers changed the nature of the Rockefeller Institute's work. The institute shifted its role from being host to a wide variety of topics, with the topics determined largely by the changing interests of guest fellows and state officials, to being a specialist in several loosely connected areas. And the substantive connection among activities was no longer New York State but states in general—as well as regions, municipalities, and communities—and especially their fiscal and institutional capacities. In fact, New York's issues were now approached more carefully and reluctantly than any other state's. To help keep the institute and SUNY out of the partisan tone of divided government in Albany, the tendency was to avoid research on New York State (except for the Center for New York State and Local Government Affairs). Gold once described his office ironically as the "Center for the Study of Forty-Nine States" (personal communication, Dec. 20, 1999).

The changes Nathan made bore some resemblance to what came before. The centers were staffed by senior faculty members from SUNY campuses. However, they were now permanent directors, not guest fellows, so the new arrangements provided greater continuity. Still, at this point, the director of the institute remained a part-timer and SUNY faculty member, as he still served as provost at Rockefeller College. The notion that the institute would be an intermediate institution between government, on the one hand, and the SUNY system, on the other, still contained some truth. Nonetheless, in two project areas in the early 1990s, the institute began to establish a new way of conducting its work and relating to governments and the governmental process. In the Winter Commission, it began to address a national audience of policymakers on issues of governmental capacity and governance. And in its JOBS Implementation Study, it established a basic research method by relying on national networks of state- or local-level research teams to analyze the implementation of public programs. More than any others, these initiatives began to create a new institute and a new and more complex set of relationships with governments and the political system.

The Winter Commission: A National Focus on State Government Performance. Some of the new projects retained a facilitative character that in some ways was not much different from the discussions and projects the institute had sponsored in the 1980s, though the facilitation was certainly at a different level, and it related to a set of substantive concerns that became a central part of the institute's emerging mission. Perhaps the best example of these evolving functions was the Winter Commission, one of the first projects at the institute to command a national audience. The Winter Commission was created in the early 1990s in response to the growing public, professional, and media interest in governmental reform. Following a series of papers on key issues ranging from civil service reform to minority diversity issues in the public service, the commission was formed with a prestigious list of members that included four former governors.

Public visibility for its work was a primary goal of the commission. Its strategies were designed to develop an audience and attract media attention around state governmental reform and measures that would enhance executive leadership. They included highly publicized hearings in six regions throughout the country with the participation of high-level public officials. The commission's report was eventually presented to President Clinton at the White House, and this presentation included an event at the National Press Club. The commission also worked closely with *Governing* magazine in disseminating its findings and recommendations. Fifty thousand extra copies of *Governing* were distributed featuring the Winter Commission report and sporting a commission-designed front cover.

The emphasis on dissemination stemmed from a wish on the part of the commission to share its work with public officials—especially state executives, including governors and their appointees—who could make good use of the information by advocating institutional reforms.

Although its products were more summaries of what was known about state and local governance and leadership than primary research, the focus of the materials on performance and the accessibility of the products made it possible for many of these social science findings to gain a broader audience among government officials at many different levels. For example, a major publication from the Winter Commission was *Hard Truths/Tough Choices* (Thompson, 1993), which offered a "concise compendium of suggestions for governmental reform and improvement aimed at rejuvenating state and local government performance and service" (Walters, 1995, p. 2).

The report offered ten sets of recommendations, ranging from strengthening executive authority to encouraging greater citizen participation in

government, on what state and local governments could do to improve performance. In an effort to assist in government reform activities, the commission offered challenge grants through a competitive process to states and
localities. These grants were meant to continue the dialogue and "build on
those efforts to achieve high-performance government" (Walters, 1995,
p. 2). The commission's recommendations sparked focused dialogue and
action at the grantee's state and local levels.

**The JOBS Study: A Research Style and a Focus on Implementa-
tion.** As the Winter Commission helped develop a national audience for
the institute and a focus on governing institutions, another project conducted in the early 1990s extended this substantive focus on institutions
and helped establish a method of conducting primary research. Although
not limited to a single research approach, the institute has come to rely
extensively on the field network evaluation methodology for collecting and
analyzing data. Developed and used by Nathan (1982) in studies conducted
at Princeton University and the Brookings Institution, the approach is flexible and adaptive. It focuses on the analysis of qualitative changes in programs or institutions, where the data collection and much of the initial
analyses are conducted by state or local field research teams. Knowledge of
and access to a particular jurisdiction allows the indigenous researchers
greater understanding of how new interventions affect a state or locality and
its public institutions and their operations. Thus, outside scholars continue
to play a key role at the institute, but they are no longer limited to SUNY
faculty.

One of the first large-scale studies conducted at the institute following
Nathan's arrival as director was a ten-state study of the implementation of
the Job Opportunities and Basic Skills (JOBS) training program, the employment program for recipients of Aid to Families with Dependent Children
created by the Family Support Act of 1988. Over three years, the Rockefeller Institute collected data from ten states using a field researcher in each
state who was familiar with its history and culture and had access to state
and local welfare systems. Jan Hagen and Irene Lurie, faculty members at
SUNY-Albany, were the principal investigators.

Hagen and Lurie (1994) concluded that the JOBS program was generally
well designed; states were increasing their spending on welfare programs and
developing their capacity to engage welfare recipients in education and training activities. They also found that JOBS provided states with critical support
services such as child care and transportation. States had also expanded working relationships with other service providers.

Despite these signs of progress, the study found that implementation
was far from complete and that some of the problems were unlikely to be
resolved soon. At the time of the study's final evaluation, most states had
not yet achieved the federally mandated goal of a 20 percent program participation rate for the welfare caseload. Hagen and Lurie (1994) concluded
that funding constraints had hampered implementation in all the major

service components, including providing educational services, child care, transportation, and staffing. Because states were implementing JOBS in a period of economic recession, they lacked the capacity to draw down federal funds for the program. At the same time, the national unemployment rate was rising and, with it, welfare caseloads increased (by 19 percent between 1990 and 1992).

Hagen and Lurie recommended a significant increase in the funding of the JOBS program for program components and staffing, but also for transitional services such as child care for low-income families recently off welfare. Other recommendations included allowing states more time to implement JOBS, a complex program with many components and challenges, including the development of information systems to support the work. The authors saw front-line workers as a large untapped resource: these workers generally supported the goals of the new legislation, but needed training, and case managers needed manageable caseloads. Both changes, the authors predicted, could yield a more effective workforce and higher-quality work.

Policymakers at the state and federal levels were interested in the results of the JOBS study, and the principal investigators testified before the U.S. Congress twice. The committees they testified before wanted to hear how the states were doing in their implementation of JOBS and what the barriers were. Lessons learned from the study of JOBS were presented in other venues as well: to the U.S. Department of Health and Human Services in 1991, 1993, and 1994; to the staff of Presidential Working Group on Welfare Reform; and to the National Governors Association Committee on Human Resources. At the state level, Lurie testified before the New York Senate Social Services and Cities committees in 1992 as well as other states.

Current Structure and Roles

Taken together, the JOBS Implementation Study and the Winter Commission gave the institute a national audience. These projects, along with those conducted in the other centers, established a more stable and potentially cumulative base of expertise—one that generally centered around implementation, program performance, administrative capacity, and fiscal change at the state and local levels. And they expressed a particular style of doing business—by relying on nationwide networks of public policy scholars in multiple disciplines (though usually in political science and economics) to conduct rich qualitative and (to a lesser degree) quantitative analyses of institutional changes; or, in the case of the Winter Commission, drawing on national networks outside academia to articulate critical issues and build political support for reforms that have been well researched but not widely adopted.

In 1998, the SUNY trustees eliminated the requirement that the director of the institute also be provost of Rockefeller College, thereby giving the institute full-time leadership. And the internal organization of the institute began to change, as the center directors were replaced with persons without teaching appointments at a SUNY campus and as new entities were established with full-time program directors. The institute can no longer be said to be anything like an intermediary or facilitator between the SUNY system and New York State government. Although it continues to work with the state government and faculty and administrators in the state university, it does so as extensions of its own mission of increasing the capacity of state and local governments, their ability to work together and with the federal government, and public awareness of the importance of implementation and administrative institutions.

Center for the Study of the States. The oldest component of the institute, and still one of the three largest groups, is the Center for the Study of the States. Before he joined the Rockefeller Institute, Steven Gold was the director of fiscal studies at the National Conference of State Legislators. From the beginning, the center focused on state fiscal issues and conducted analyses and published reports for all states. In August 1990, the first State Revenue Report was published. A quarterly analysis of tax revenue collections in the fifty states, it quickly found a wide audience in both the financial and general media.

At first, most of the work at the center focused on secondary data analysis for all states, although some case studies looked at smaller samples of states in greater depth using primary data. Major projects included public school financing in the United States and Canada and state spending trends on programs for children. The center also published frequent fiscal briefs on various fiscal issues facing states, including state and local revenue systems, state governments and fiscal trends, and state tax cuts. These materials found a wide audience in the private and public sectors. The reports were also widely used by the nonprofit and advocate community, the national press, and academics.

In 1995, Donald Boyd became director of the Center for the Study of the States. Boyd continued the center's basic publications and reports and added new relationships with a number of New York State agencies. Boyd had many contacts in state government from his years working at the Division of Budget, and the center's reputation made it possible for it to reestablish direct ties with the state government. By hiring the Rockefeller Institute for large analytical tasks, state agencies were able to contract the work out of house but not "out of neighborhood."

Federalism Research Group. The Federalism Research Group was established in 1996 to analyze state and local responses to the devolution of social programs. Its focus is on the changing institutions of welfare, health care, workforce development programs, and other social services and states' capacities to manage these programs. The group is directed by Thomas Gais, a political scientist.

The group's major project has been the Capacity Study. In the winter following enactment of the Personal Responsibility and Work Opportunity

Act of 1996, the Rockefeller Institute launched this multistate analysis of the management systems for welfare and related programs. The study used the field research network to collect data on the policy choices and management activities in nineteen states as they implemented new welfare systems in order to comply with the 1996 federal requirements and their own welfare reforms. A field research director in each state used a standardized report form to gather and analyze qualitative and quantitative information from the state and two local field sites on how states were assigning roles to different types of agencies, the capacities of their information systems, the distribution of responsibility and power between state and local offices, the role of private contractors, and the effects of these changes on the operations of local welfare agencies.

The study's reports have been widely distributed and discussed by officials at all levels of government. Its findings that the states lacked the capacity to adapt their information systems to the new case management and program planning needs of the new work-based welfare eventually led to the creation of the Working Seminar on Information Systems for Social Programs, a joint program by the institute and the U.S. General Accounting Office (GAO). In turn, the working seminar eventually led GAO to conduct a joint research effort with the institute on the status and capacities of welfare information systems.

The basic findings of the Capacity Study also led to several other projects and research efforts. The Front-Line Management and Practices Study, funded by the U.S. Department of Health and Human Services and conducted by Irene Lurie and Norma Riccucci of SUNY-Albany and Marcia Meyers of Columbia University, is examining program signals, service access, and other aspects of welfare implementation by directly observing interactions between welfare workers and clients. The Fiscal Effects Study, although part of the Capacity Study, is being conducted by the Center for the Study of the States. It is examining the effects of welfare reform on social service spending by the states, and it is designed to give state officials, communities, advocacy groups, and federal officials a good understanding of the overall fiscal impacts of the 1996 block grant. It has already released a four-state pilot study of changes in spending levels and priorities before and after the implementation of the Personal Responsibility Act. Still other studies include an analysis of Medicaid managed care programs and states' capacity to oversee and enforce contracts with managed care organizations and an analysis of the implementation of the Workforce Investment Act. Finally, although the Capacity Study is not focused on New York State, the institute conducted New York's study of welfare "leavers" in cooperation with the responsible state agencies, and it is working with the City of New York on analyzing its welfare management systems.

Urban and Metropolitan Studies Group. The Urban and Metropolitan Studies Group was founded in 1995 and has been directed ever since by David Wright, former top aide to Governor Mario Cuomo. Rather than focus on policy implementation and management, the group uses the field research evaluation methodology to draw a more complete picture of urban neighborhoods. Its current work is the Study of Urban Neighborhood and Community Capacity Building, which identifies nonpoor majority-minority neighborhoods and defines the forces that influence the character and shape of these neighborhoods over time. With data drawn from the field over the course of these several studies, the Urban Group has begun to define aspects of social capital in communities and how they can influence neighborhood change. Field researchers have begun to isolate the forces in the study communities that seem to function as resiliency factors in the face of negative neighborhood change. These strengths at the neighborhood level may operate as deterrents to the negative pressures that have pushed other communities into downward spirals of danger and distress, fueling the negative stereotypes of urban neighborhoods. In developing this area of work, the institute places high priority on its teaching mission. Part of its goal is to communicate the information from its work with the larger community of policy scholars and practitioners. Conclusions from this work counter myths and stereotypes commonly held about urban neighborhoods.

Other Programs. Other programs reinforce the institute's expertise in program performance and institutional change. The Center for the Effectiveness in Higher Education, directed by a former SUNY provost and interim chancellor, Joseph C. Burke, conducts research on the impacts and implementation of performance funding initiatives for state universities and other public institutions for higher education. Dall Forsythe, a former New York State budget director, is also studying performance management and budgeting as he leads a national commission established by the Pew Charitable Trust, the Task Force on Performance Management. This project is a broad inquiry into the status and effects of new and changing systems of performance management by federal, state, and local governments. It has focused thus far on the pilot phase of the federal program stemming from the Government Performance and Results Act of 1993, an initiative to improve management by federal agencies.

Conclusion

Although the growing independence of the Rockefeller Institute has given it a role very different from its original mission of being a facilitative institution between New York State government and the SUNY system, these developments were hardly accidental and seem to reflect important features of modern government and academia. Developing the institute's own expertise and substantive focus was necessary to engage in the large-scale analyses of public sector change now needed to contribute to the public debate, where an enormous number of private think tanks, associations, and advocacy organizations are competing for the attention of government officials. The institute's focus on management systems, governance, and institutional change allows it to sidestep most ideological debates and permits it to maintain a neutral, nonpartisan stance even when making strong statements about the implementation of highly divisive policies. If there is any one conclusion to be drawn from the early history of the institute, it is that the rapid pace of change in the public sector and the complex ways in which those changes play out at the subnational level make it difficult for academicians in the normal course of their work to play an important advisory role to government officials and stakeholders. That difficulty argues for greater specialization, autonomy, and continuity in university think tanks.

References

Hagen, J., and Lurie, I. *Implementing Jobs: Progress and Promise.* Albany, N.Y.: Nelson A. Rockefeller Institute of Government, 1994.

Nathan, R. P. "The Methodology for Field Network Evaluation Studies." In W. Williams (ed.), *Studying Implementation: Methodological and Administrative Issues.* Chatham, N.J.: Chatham House, 1982.

Nelson A. Rockefeller Institute of Government. *New York State Project 2000: Economic Development.* Albany, N.Y.: Nelson A. Rockefeller Institute of Government, 1986.

Nelson A. Rockefeller Institute of Government. *Overview.* Albany, N.Y.: Nelson A. Rockefeller Institute of Government, 1999.

Thompson, F. J. (ed.). *Hard Truths/Tough Choices: An Agenda for State and Local Reform.* Albany, N.Y.: Nelson A. Rockefeller Institute of Government, 1993.

Walters, J. *Paths to Performance: A Seven State Focus.* Albany, N.Y.: Nelson A. Rockefeller Institute of Government, 1995.

For Further Reading

Benjamin, G., and Dullea, H. N. (eds.). *Decision 1997: Constitutional Change in New York.* Albany, N.Y.: Nelson A. Rockefeller Institute of Government, 1997.

Burke, J. C., and Modarresi, S. *Performance Funding and Budgeting: Popularity and Volatility—The Third Annual Survey.* Albany, N.Y.: Nelson A. Rockefeller Institute of Government, 1999.

Burke, J. C., Modarresi, S., and Serban, A. "Performance: Shouldn't It Count for Something?" *Change Magazine,* 1999, *31*(6), 16–23.

Ellwood, D. A., and Boyd, D. J. *Changes in State Spending on Social Services Since the Implementation of Welfare Reform.* Albany, N.Y.: Nelson A. Rockefeller Institute of Government, 2000.

Fossett, J. W., and others. *Managing Accountability in Medicaid Managed Care: The Politics of Public Management.* Albany, N.Y.: Nelson A. Rockefeller Institute of Government, 1999.

Gold, S. D. (ed.). *The Fiscal Crisis of the States: Lessons for the Future.* Washington, D.C.: Georgetown University Press, 1995.

Gold, S. D., and Liebschutz, D. S. *State Tax Relief for the Poor.* (2nd ed.) Albany, N.Y.: Nelson A. Rockefeller Institute of Government, 1996.

Gold, S. D., Smith, D. M., and Lawton, S. B. (eds.). *Public School Finance Programs of the United States and Canada, 1993–1994.* Albany, N.Y.: Nelson A. Rockefeller Institute of Government, 1995.

Lurie, I. "Field Network Studies." Paper presented at the Implementation Evaluation Methods Conference, Bethesda, Md., May 14–15, 1999.

Malbin, M. J., and Gais, T. L. *The Day After Reform: Sobering Campaign Finance Lessons from the American States.* Albany, N.Y.: Nelson A. Rockefeller Institute of Government, 1998.

Maxwell, T. "Welfare Reform and Information Management: Rewiring the Human Service System." *Rockefeller Reports,* Dec. 5, 1997, pp. 1–7.

Meyers, M. K. "Gaining Cooperation at the Front Lines of Service Delivery: Issues for the Implementation of Welfare Reform." *Rockefeller Reports,* Apr. 30, 1998, pp. 1–7.

Nathan, R. P. "What Next for the Public Service?" *Rockefeller Institute Bulletin,* 1991, pp. 16–20.

Nathan, R. P. "The Newest New Federalism for Welfare: Where Are We Now and Where Are We Headed?" *Rockefeller Reports,* July 25, 1997, pp. 1–8.

Nathan, R. P., and Gais, T. L. *Implementing the Personal Responsibility Act of 1996: A First Look.* Albany, N.Y.: Nelson A. Rockefeller Institute of Government, 1999.

Nelson A. Rockefeller Institute of Government. *After Welfare: A Study of Work and Benefit Use After Case Closing.* Albany, N.Y.: Nelson A. Rockefeller Institute of Government, 1999.

Nelson A. Rockefeller Institute of Government. *Information Federalism: History of Welfare Information Systems.* Albany, N.Y.: Nelson A. Rockefeller Institute of Government, 1999.

Owens, M. L., and Wright, D. J. "The Diversity of Majority-Black Neighborhoods." *Rockefeller Institute Bulletin,* 1998, pp. 78–86.

Thompson, F. J. (ed.). *Revitalizing State and Local Public Service: Strengthening Performance, Accountability, and Citizen Confidence.* San Francisco: Jossey-Bass, 1993.

U.S. General Accounting Office. *Welfare Reform: Improving State Automated Systems Requires Coordinated Federal Effort.* Washington, D.C: Government Printing Office, 2000.

U.S. House of Representatives. Committee on Ways and Means. *Oversight of Welfare Reform: Hearing Before the Subcommittee on Human Resources.* 105th Cong., 2nd sess., Mar. 19, 1998.

Wright, D. J. *Comprehensive Strategies for Community Renewal.* Albany, N.Y.: Nelson A. Rockefeller Institute of Government, 1997.

Wright, D. J. "Saving City Neighborhoods: New Findings, Trends and Policies." *Rockefeller Institute Bulletin,* 1999, pp. 90–102.

THOMAS GAIS is the director of the Federalism Research Group at the Nelson A. Rockefeller Institute of Government at the State University of New York, Albany..

CATHERINE LAWRENCE is a research associate at the Nelson A. Rockefeller Institute of Government.

8

A distinguishing purpose of this university policy institute is to foster civic engagement on a wide variety of local and state issues.

The Reubin O'Donovan Askew Institute: Building Community in Florida

David R. Colburn, Lynn H. Leverty

Established in the spring of 1994 at the University of Florida, the Reubin O'Donovan Askew Institute on Politics and Society has focused its energies on reinvigorating civic culture and revitalizing community building in Florida. The founders of the institute, led by the state's former governor, Reubin O'Donovan Askew, decided that Florida's principal need was not in the area of public policy research and training programs, but in finding ways to improve the state's civic culture. The engagement of citizens in public life had deteriorated throughout the second half of the twentieth century as new residents entered the state at a rate that often exceeded 650 people per day, as different ethnic and racial groups immigrated to Florida, and as regional differences were sharpened by the settlement patterns of these new residents. The founders of the institute viewed the deterioration of community and civic discourse and the increased ethnic and racial hostility in Florida as detrimental to the health of its democracy and to the future of the state and its citizens.

Civic Culture in Florida

Concerns about the decline of civic culture and community vitality in Florida are not new. As early as 1949, political scientist V. O. Key Jr., in his work *Southern Politics in State and Nation,* titled his chapter on Florida, "Every Man for Himself." Key argued that the state was socially fragmented and politically balkanized as a result of immigration, geography, a regionalized economy, and a "dispersed" political leadership. Subsequent analysts, including Manning Dauer (1972), David Colburn and Richard Scher (1980), and David Colburn and Lance deHaven-Smith (1999), found that the fragmentation in the state had worsened over time. The pressures of in-migration, immigration, economic regionalization, geographical isolation, and the proliferation of gated communities had led former Governor Lawton Chiles (1995) to observe that Florida had become "more of a crowd than a community" (p. 6).

The decline of civic culture in Florida is not unique. Concerns about the deterioration of civic culture and community have gained both academic and popular attention in recent years. John Gardner has been among the most forceful advocates for a nationwide effort to revitalize community and civic culture "Without the community of shared values that community provides," Gardner argued, "freedom cannot survive." He warned Americans, "Freedom is not a natural condition. Habeas corpus, trial by jury, a free press and all other practices that ensure our freedom are social constructions" (1991, p. 5).

Florida's Evolution in the Twentieth Century

Civic discourse between citizens of Florida and their political representatives has suffered tremendously because of the dramatic changes that occurred in the state during the twentieth century. Florida is only barely recognizable as the southern state that languished behind most of the rest of the nation and the region at the beginning of the twentieth century. In less than one hundred years, Florida has evolved from the smallest state in the South, with slightly more than 500,000 residents, to the largest, with nearly 15.5 million people. In 1900 most Floridians lived within fifty miles of the Georgia border in what was largely a southern, rural, agricultural, and frontierlike society. Jacksonville was the largest city with 28,249 residents, Pensacola stood a distant second with 17,747 citizens, and Miami had only 1,681 residents. Squatters inhabited much of south Florida, substantial portions of which appeared uninhabitable. Race dominated social and political relations in the state during this period, and Florida followed southern customs by passing laws to segregate the races and creating a one-party political system to ensure white dominance.

By 2000, Florida had become the fourth largest state in the nation, with one of the most urban as well as the most racially and ethnically diverse populations in the nation. Agriculture and fishing have been replaced by tourism, and international commerce and technology have become increasingly prominent. Perhaps more symbolically, Florida is the launch site for space exploration, and Miami serves as both the financial and cultural capital of the Caribbean.

The rapid changes of the past one hundred years have come with significant costs for the state's civic culture. A resident of rural Taylor County

captured the sentiments of north Florida in 1993 when he commented,"
We're a southern state and damn proud of it" (Colburn and deHaven-Smith,
1999, p. 6). But three hundred miles to the south, a resident of Dade County
looked thoroughly bewildered when asked what it meant to be a southerner.
Despite the claim of the Taylor County resident, fewer than half the state's
residents had lived in Florida prior to 1970, and more Floridians had been
born in New York than in any other state, excluding Florida.

The demographic changes in Florida during the past century have complicated the crisis over identity among its citizens. For much of its recent
history, Florida has been essentially two states: one that extends south from
the Georgia border to just south of Ocala and that has identified with the
South and its social, political, and racial traditions, and the other that
extends north from Key West and Miami to just north of Orlando, with a
heritage that has little connection to the South, has historically had a diverse
ethnic and racial population, and has viewed the state as part of a national
and international economy. The consequence has been that Floridians have
little sense of their own identity, and few issues unify them as a people. The
residents of Orlando, for example, believe they have little in common with
the Latin residents of Miami or the Crackers who reside in north Florida.
Tourism and the mega-theme parks such as Disney World shape their
worldview. Residents of Miami similarly have little sense of north Florida
and its residents and see them as potential enemies rather than as neigh-
bors. The absence of a statewide identity occasionally reaches the mundane
in the state. For example, Floridians are free to purchase license plates that
highlight their interests (panthers, manatees, public education, higher education, veterans, and other areas). One humorist commented that Floridians are so divided that they cannot even agree about the design of their
license plate.

Complicating this picture has been the heavy migration of seniors into
the state, who view Florida as little more than a retirement haven (Colburn
and deHaven-Smith, 1999, p. 50). Senator Bob Graham has referred to this
phenomenon as the "Cincinnati factor": retired citizens move to Florida but
continue to think of themselves as residents of Cincinnati, subscribe to a
Cincinnati paper, often vacation in Ohio, and ship their remains to Cincinnati to be buried (p. 33). Most also have little or no perspective on Florida's
history or development and the consequences such development has had
for the state and local communities. Moreover, they have little interest in
such a perspective. They are generally resistant to new government initiatives and programs that will change the status quo, cost more money, or
require additional taxes.

As an increasing number of native whites feel beleaguered by the
changes in their state and less in control of a society that they perceive as
their own, sociologists have observed the resurgence of white ethnicity. The
development of this ethnic identity has been particularly true in north Florida, where the growing diversity of the state's population has heightened

concerns among whites. Recently a barber in Gainesville, who is also a native of north Florida, reflected the concerns of white natives when he commented that Miami "is not a city in Florida, it is a foreign country" (Colburn and deHaven-Smith, 1999, p. 76). The concerns among whites have been intensified by the tendency among Cuban and black residents to vote as blocs on candidates and issues. Although this is a historic pattern in the United States that was also common for most whites and white immigrant groups in the nineteenth and twentieth centuries, subsequent generations of whites have tended to forget their own history in this regard and the reasons that minority groups congeal as voting blocs.

The trend toward a more diverse Florida shows no sign of abating. Immigrants have made Florida one of their four major immigrant gateways in the United States (the others are California, Texas, and New York). In 1995, demographer Douglas Massey argued that the nation is witnessing an age of "perpetual immigration" in which immigrants from Latin America and Asia are continually "augmented by a steady supply of fresh arrivals from abroad" (p. 643). Florida's Hispanic and Latino population, for example, is projected to reach 24 percent of the state's population, or 5 million people, in 2025, even if Fidel Castro should fall from power and many Cubans opt to return to their native land.

Community building and civic culture are further endangered in Florida by the fragmented nature of state politics. The architects of the state constitution in both 1885 and 1968 ensured that there would be no center of gravity in the state's political system and no one institution where either responsibility or authority was fixed. Members of the cabinet are elected separately and share decision-making responsibility with the governor. This situation was modified, but not significantly changed, by the 1998 revisions to the Constitution. Individual or group power tends to count for much more than a concern for the common good in the state. Single-member districts, adopted in 1980, contribute to the balkanization of state politics. While this change in representation has facilitated the election of black representatives, it has tended to isolate black and white voters from one another.

Development of the Askew Institute

The way Florida residents harmonize this diversity and govern themselves now stimulates a great deal of interest in the state. But creating a healthy civic culture and constructing a new statewide identity for Florida is by no means certain. Concerns about this situation and its consequences for the state's future motivated former Governor Reubin O'Donovan Askew to establish the Askew Institute at the University of Florida. During his eight years in office, from 1971 to 1979, Askew did much to modernize Florida and to draw public attention to issues that were critical to the state's future. In particular, he engaged citizens in a public discourse about a host of crucial issues confronting the state, including school busing and the integration of Florida's public schools, protection of its environment, tax reform, and public ethics and open government. The Askew Institute is an extension of his commitment as governor to civic engagement. In the spring of 1994, Askew agreed to the formation of the institute in his name at the University of Florida and the establishment of an annual Askew Forum, designed to open a dialogue between Floridians and scholars about critical issues facing the state.

The Askew Institute is also a natural extension of the University of Florida's role as a land grant institution. One of its aims is to make the abstract and theoretical research of faculty available to state and local leaders so that it can be used to sustain and enrich Florida's social, economic, and political environment. The institute's annual meeting and annual report bring the relevant research of faculty in history, economics, political science, sociology, and public policy to the attention of policy leaders and citizens.

Annual Meeting of the Institute

The Reubin O'Donovan Askew Institute began holding annual statewide forums in the fall of 1995 on the campus of the University of Florida. The three primary goals of the institute's annual meeting have remained unchanged over the five years of its existence: (1) to gather thoughtful men and women together to converse with one another about the critical issues facing Florida, (2) to explore the past for insights into the future, and (3) to begin restoring a civic culture in Florida by providing a forum in which fundamental issues can be addressed by citizens in a bipartisan manner. These meetings bring together about 175 men and women who are actively involved in state and local affairs and to engage them in the process of strengthening the state's civic culture. Participants include faculty from the state's universities and community colleges, state and local officials, representatives from other statewide organizations, the news and broadcasting media, and members of the business and nonprofit communities. Most, if not all, of these people are well informed about the issues confronting Florida. The institute seeks to broaden and deepen their understanding of the issues under consideration, draw on their considerable expertise to develop a process to address critical issues, and engage them in enhancing civic engagement with other Floridians when they return to their communities.

A related purpose of the annual meeting is to strengthen the general quality of leadership in the state and provide an opportunity for leaders and citizens from all sectors of society to interact and to think about the future needs of Florida. The institute has no formal program to develop community leaders, but by bringing representatives from diverse groups as well as interested citizens together each year, it provides them with the opportunity to network with people who have a deep commitment to the state's future. The Askew Institute also works closely with Leadership Florida and other organizations at the community level that train state and local leaders so that they too will understand the state's recent history, the deterioration of its democracy, and the issues that threaten to divide Floridians further. Finally, the institute informs participants about how they can remain actively involved in addressing the issues of the annual meeting when they return to their communities.

Each annual Askew Institute meeting begins by reexamining the enduring ideas and traditions that have shaped the United States and Florida and reminding participants of the fundamental importance of these traditions in developing solutions to problems. The purpose of this approach is to provide participants with a philosophical perspective and also to encourage them to think about policy concerns within the context of those principles that remain fundamental to American democracy. In addition, the institute provides a brief historical overview of the topic under discussion at each annual meeting so that participants have an understanding of how the issues evolved over time.

During the past five years the Askew Institute has examined the following topics: "Building Community at the State and Local Levels in Florida," "What Floridians Will Expect from State Government in the Twenty-First Century," "Florida and the Global Economy," "A View of the Twenty-First Century: Demographic Developments and Their Implications for Florida's Future," and "The Graying of Florida."

Following each meeting, the Askew Institute has published an annual report summarizing the proceedings, featuring the recommendations of the participants, highlighting the comments of the keynote speakers, offering readers a perspective on the topic by highlighting one or more of the papers prepared for the meeting, and providing readers with additional references about the topic so that they can inform themselves further about it. The recommendations and the report are meant to capture the thinking of participants and to open up avenues for public discourse at the state and community levels. They are not necessarily policy proposals.

From the first meeting in 1995, topics have been chosen that are critical to the state and its future. Community building has remained an underlying theme of each meeting. For example, during the 1998 meeting, "Florida and the Global Economy," it was evident that only residents of selected areas of the state (generally south Florida and the major urban areas) have been engaged in the process of globalization and have considered the consequences of economic globalization for Florida. Organizers of the conference and participants were concerned that globalization would fragment the state further if a concerted effort was not made to keep citizens informed and engaged about global developments and Florida's involvement in them. Since that meeting, economic and business leaders have pursued a variety of initiatives to expand citizen awareness of the global economy and to involve other regions in this global outreach.

At the 1999 and 2000 meetings, the Askew Institute has invited participants and Floridians to begin thinking about the state's future. If the twentieth century posed a significant challenge to the state's civic culture, the twenty-first promises to compound it and add its own set of challenges. Florida's projected population growth is expected to average 550 people per day for the next twenty-five years, and its population is projected to reach 20.7 million, making it the third largest state in the nation. Although projections that Florida's population will become increasingly more diverse in the twenty-first century have significant implications for the state, it will not be the most significant demographic development in the state's future. By the year 2025, Florida's senior population is expected to exceed 26 percent of the population and exercise the dominant voice in public policy-making.

The 1999 meeting asked participants to examine the implications of the state's population growth through 2025 in the areas of economic development, education, health care, crime, and racial and ethnic diversity. Participants agreed that the state must focus on community building, establishing a stronger educational system from early childhood to graduate school, constructing and maintaining a better economic infrastructure, providing programs to assist families, and enhancing communication at all levels of society if Floridians are to prosper in the new century.

The 2000 meeting focused on Florida's senior citizens. Florida's senior population is already larger than the populations of seventeen states. The continued growth of this segment of the population has significant implications for policy, especially in the areas of health care, transportation, and social programs, as well as in community building and civic discourse. Increasingly seniors are residing in separate communities unconnected even to the cities in which they are located. In Marion County, near Ocala, for example, a retirement residential community is currently under construction to house fifteen thousand seniors; children and younger adults may visit but cannot live there. This retirement community will be gated and will meet nearly all of its own needs, from recreation to health care, social programs, and religious services. In essence it will become a community within the community of Ocala, but residents will have little sense of belonging to Ocala. This model has been (and is being) increasingly replicated in other parts of the state. The concern in Florida is that these seniors will have little interest in addressing the needs of the larger community because so many of their needs are satisfied within their own retirement communities.

Seniors have a track record of voting in much higher percentages than members of other age groups, so the great concern is that they will oppose measures that address other state needs, especially if financial costs are attached to them. The U.S. Census Bureau and Division of Elections found in the 1998 elections that seniors constituted 18 percent of the state's population, 24 percent of the voting-age population, and 27 percent of the state's registered voters. Moreover, political scientist Susan McManus (1998) noted that exit surveys of the 1998 gubernatorial election revealed that seniors represented 32 percent of all voters. And when those age sixty and older were lumped together, they represented a staggering 42 percent of the voters. Moreover, seniors increasingly are electing their own to local and county government posts. For example, seniors constitute 29 percent of the city council members in Florida compared to 23 percent nationally.

The Askew Institute seeks to engage seniors in a discourse about the needs of the state and all its citizens. The concern is that if seniors are not engaged, they will remain focused on their own needs and their own world, and unreceptive to the desires of the larger community. The result will be a generational divide that almost certainly will become the state's major political battleground.

Local Communities and the Askew Institute

In an effort to promote community building and greater civic engagement in regional and local issues, the Askew Institute has begun offering programs at the community level. The first such meeting took place in Jacksonville on October 8, 1999, and examined the topic, "How to Ensure Smart Growth for Jacksonville." Using the format developed for the annual statewide meeting, the institute focused on developing civic leadership through education and public discussion. The institute will be holding two to three local conferences each year, in addition to the statewide conference, to help stimulate civic engagement between local government and residents.

Broadening civic discourse in a state as large and diverse as Florida is beyond the scope of any one organization. For this reason, the Askew Institute has also been working with other state organizations to strengthen the conversation about democracy in Florida. These organizations include the Florida Institute of Government, the LeRoy Collins Center for Public Policy, Leadership Florida, Florida Tax Watch, the Florida Humanities Council, the Askew School on Public Policy at the Florida State University, and the Florida Council of 100. Representatives from these organizations sit on the Askew Executive Committee and meet at least once a year to discuss the annual meeting and work with the Askew Institute on other initiatives. The goal with each of these organizations has been to coordinate programs and cooperate in areas where the Askew Institute can assist in enhancing civic life in Florida.

Most recently, the Askew Institute, the Collins Center, Leadership Florida, and the Askew School cooperated with a community-building effort in the Tampa Bay region. Called "Hillsborough Tomorrow," this citizen initiative has sought to find ways to address issues that affect the entire region, from roads to schools to air and water quality. A view from the air suggests, in fact, that the entire region is interconnected and that boundaries between communities are no longer obvious. Hillsborough Tomorrow has been a challenging effort for local citizens and for those from various public policy institutes because it attempts to reach beyond local governments to address regional needs. Persuading local leaders to rise above local concerns, however, has required the stamina of a long-distance runner and the patience of Job.

New Initiatives at the Askew Institute

Fragmentation has been characteristic not only of the state's civic and political culture but also of the relationships between local governments. The Askew Institute has developed a Web page (www.clas.ufl.edu.askew/) that identifies on-line resources to assist local governments. In recent years, many local governments have had to cut back or eliminate research staff, which has reduced their ability to plan and respond to the changing needs of their communities. Resources exist within the state to help these communities fill their research needs, but there is no organized way for local officials to find these resources. The Askew Web page includes the resources of the state university system research centers and faculty (for example, survey capability, program evaluation, planning, program facilitation, and similar services). It also provides links to census data and other data sets and information on state and federal resources, foundation information, training conferences, and grant availability.

Related to this initiative, the institute is conducting a survey of two hundred Florida communities concerning local community-building efforts. The survey will provide a clearer picture of local efforts to promote civic participation and to resolve conflict and of processes that seem to be working. Results of the survey will be shared with communities across the state.

Conclusion

During the first five years of its existence, the Askew Institute has accomplished many of its original aims and is now beginning to fashion new ones. With this in mind, the institute has focused on three areas of interest and concern:

The effort to build community in Florida has been enormously complicated by the state's rapid rate of growth. How can the institute help communities in Florida address issues of civic engagement when population change is so constant?

Efforts by the Askew Institute to bring scholars and public policy leaders together have met with only marginal success. Although many University of Florida faculty are involved in the institute, the intent was to bring together faculty from throughout the state university system. What additional steps can the institute take to enhance the interaction between faculty and public policy leaders and to encourage faculty involvement in addressing state problems?

How does the Askew Institute meet the challenge of addressing major issues confronting Florida at its annual meeting without appearing to be superficial and trendy in its approach? What steps can it take to ensure that these issues are engaged substantively over time?

The institute is wrestling with answers to these questions, which are central to its evolution and future plans.

The challenges facing Florida's future and the health of its democracy are significant by any measure. A large, diverse, and graying population with a multicultural background has made it more difficult to build consensus and promote civic discourse, but it also makes it essential that this work be done. While recognizing the obstacles confronting the state, the Askew Institute believes that Florida is important and fertile ground for democratic renewal. If states like Florida fail in promoting civic discourse, we cannot be sanguine about the future of American democracy.

References

Chiles, L. W. *Building Community in Florida: A Report on the 1995 Meeting of the Reubin O'Donovan Askew Institute on Politics and Society, November 1995.* Gainesville: Reubin O'Donovan Askew Institute.

Colburn, D. R., and deHaven-Smith, L. *Government in the Sunshine State.* Gainesville: University Presses of Florida, 1999.

Colburn, D. R., and Scher, R. K. *Florida's Gubernatorial Politics in the Twentieth Century.* Gainesville: University Presses of Florida, 1980.

Dauer, M. "Florida: The Different State." In W. Harvard (ed.), *The Changing Politics of the South.* Baton Rouge: Louisiana State Press, 1972.

Gardner, J. W. *Building Community.* Washington, D.C.: INDEPENDENT SECTOR, 1991.

Key, V. O., Jr. *Southern Politics in State and Nation.* New York: Vintage Books, 1949.

McManus, S. A. "Retiree Recruitment: How Florida's Burgeoning Senior Population Is Transforming State and Local Politics." *Responses to an Aging Population,* Fall 1998.

Massey, D. S. "The New Immigration and Ethnicity in the United States." *Population and Development Review,* 1995, 2, 631–652.

DAVID R. COLBURN *is director of the Reubin O'Donovan Askew Institute at the University of Florida and provost of the university.*

LYNN H. LEVERTY *is associate director of the Askew Institute and a member of the political science faculty at the University of Florida.*

9

The Humphrey Institute focuses on redesigning institutions as a way of resolving public policy issues.

The Humphrey Institute: Designing Institutions of Governance

John E. Brandl, G. Edward Schuh

The Humphrey Institute has become a very different organization from its original predecessor at the University of Minnesota, the Public Administration Center. Formed in 1933 as one of America's first academic units for the education of civil servants, the Public Administration Center was heavily influenced by the writings of Woodrow Wilson, who had posited a distinction between policy and administration. While some people did both, others carried out the wishes of policymakers by pursuing administration.

Over fifty years later, in the late 1960s, there developed a widespread perception that public administration centers needed revamping. They were seen by many as intellectual adjuncts of political science departments, in need of invigoration from other relevant academic disciplines. In the curriculum of the University of Minnesota's School of Public Affairs, formed in 1968 from the previous Public Administration Center, economics and statistics held pride of place. Here as elsewhere, it was increasingly clear by the 1970s or 1980s that policy analysis alone was insufficient preparation for public service. At Minnesota, management was given greater emphasis in the curriculum. Meanwhile, a small planning program had been relocated from the School of Architecture to the School of Public Affairs at the University of Minnesota so that by the 1980s the public affairs curriculum was rooted in three areas: analysis, planning, and management.

The scope of the program changed in another important way. In its early days, it was largely a regional training program that focused primarily on state and local programs. Over time it has evolved into a program that seeks to address national and international issues; welcomes students from across the nation and internationally; and pursues research, teaching, and outreach activities in many other countries.

Financing the Institute

The institute has been innovative in how it finances its programs. In recent years only about 15 percent of its budget has come from the central resources of the university, that is, from funds appropriated by the state legislature. Another 20 percent comes from income off its endowment, and tuition accounts for 10 percent of the institute's income. These are the sources of funding for the institute's teaching programs, that is, for faculty and staff salaries and student assistance. The remainder of the budget, about half, comes from external funding.

There are twenty-three tenured or tenure-track faculty members, as well as several dozen adjunct faculty who provide the backbone of the institute. In addition, the institute uses a system of senior fellows as the basis for attracting most of its outside funds. These persons are academic entrepreneurs; their appointment in the institute is dependent on their ability to raise the funds for their activities. A senior fellow appointment is deemed to be equivalent to a full professorship. However, senior fellows do not have tenure, and their appointments continue only so long as they raise the funds to support themselves and their activities. They do, with a few exceptions, have full-time appointments.

An important strength of this system is that it protects the institute from being locked into an outdated staffing pattern as societal problems evolve, and it enables the institute to respond in a timely fashion to the needs of society. If a fellow's work becomes irrelevant, the flow of funds stops, the fellow would leave the institute, and the leadership of the institute would search for a successor with the capacity to address new or emerging problems. Another important strength of the system is that it has a built-in system of performance evaluation. A fellow's ability to attract external funding is constantly evaluated by peer reviewers and funding agencies (and by colleagues in the institute).

Raising 100 percent of one's funding, while at the same time paying the administrative costs of managing a program, is a demanding task. Nevertheless, the institute has sustained some fifteen senior fellows in recent years, and some of them have been at the institute for ten years or more. These high performers who continue to address important contemporary problems are a key strength of the institute.

Another important feature of the institute is that individual faculty and fellows organize their activities under the umbrella of centers, which are typically organized around contemporary public policy issues (examples are the Center for School Change and the International Women's Rights Action Watch). The faculty and fellows conduct research, serve as experts, and publish on the issue. This focus makes the funding of the centers attractive to outside donors, while promoting collaboration with other faculty and programs at the university. This approach has been an important means of promoting problem-oriented, multidisciplinary research and outreach programs.

Policymaking as Institutional Design

Before the 1980s, the prevailing view at the University of Minnesota and elsewhere was that policymaking was the preferred choice among policy alternatives. Under this model, analysts, planners, and managers would present a decision maker with options and the pros and cons, which had been delineated, often by cost-benefit or cost-effectiveness analysis. Implicitly the policymaker was assumed to represent the public good and to choose the appropriate option. Throughout the heyday of policy analysis in the 1960s and 1970s, many policy analysts and other scholars of public affairs knew that policy analysis was not sufficient; simply analyzing the costs and benefits of alternative policies did not necessarily yield more effective policies. However, there was not yet a widely known theoretical framework that would explain that suspicion. By the 1990s, a broader understanding of policymaking was being developed, one in which academicians did not grant omniscience and benevolence to policymakers.

For generations analysts and planners, especially those with a background in economics, had understood market failure as providing a rationale for government action. It has become apparent that governments are also prone to failure, and to failure in the same ways that markets fall short. Thus, it is not enough to identify ways in which markets are flawed. It became as essential to examine how governments might act in the face of market failures as it was to identify the cause of the market failure. Do governments regularly correct for market failures? To assume so is to depend on either spontaneous public-spiritedness of persons in government or careful oversight of government's programs. It is hard to make a case that either of those is a consistent force for accomplishing public purposes. Institutions—markets, bureaus or agencies, legislatures, schools, and others—shape the actions of persons operating within them. Depending on how they are structured, they can foster systematically beneficial or systematically deleterious behavior.

Two broad strains of thinking concerning institutions have emerged in the social sciences. The first attempts to incorporate the emergence and evolution of institutions as something to be explained endogenously by the theory, not something taken as a given or exogenous. Vernon Ruttan at the University of Minnesota is a leader among those following this approach. Ruttan's perspective is that once institutions become barriers to economic growth and development, political and economic "market" forces emerge from the society to ease the constraint implied by those institutions. The specific direction in which the institutions evolve will be shaped by the resource endowment in the particular economy, the cultural endowment of the society, and the technology available and adapted to the society (Ruttan and Hayami, 1984).

This framework can be useful in understanding how and why institutions have evolved in a particular way. It can also be valuable in designing the institutions of the future. Both political systems and economic markets are imperfect. The failure of proper institutions to emerge, the existence of unresponsive institutions, or the failure of policymakers to design proper institutions can cause failure in attaining the objectives of the governance system. On a more positive note, in designing new institutions or redesigning existing institutions, the Ruttan perspective suggests that institution designers should be shaping them to adapt to the changing resource endowment, the cultural endowment (which also may be changing), and the rapidly changing technology in our society.

The other approach to institutional design emphasizes the idea that policymakers impose their views on a situation. They make decisions. Their decisions are not to be modeled (in the sense of being predicted by forces impinging on them), either because social science does not yet have the capacity to explain behavior to that degree or because of a conviction that humans ultimately possess autonomy, free will, and the ability to make rational decisions influenced, but not determined, by outside influences.

Raising the question of how individuals will act in different situations (for example, in a competitive firm, a monopoly, a school, or government agency) leads to a broad mission for the social sciences. Understanding the behavior of individuals is critical to the design or redesign of institutional arrangements. Yet individuals act differently within different institutions. To design the institutions, one has to understand how that behavior is different under different institutions (in the market versus in a government agency, for example), and ultimately how the design of the institutions affects that behavior. In addition, we must understand how the behavior of individuals brings about changes in the institutions.

The academic field of public affairs has become the study of the design and operation of the institutions of governance. Under what circumstances and within what institutions will the actions of individuals aggregate to public good? The need for government arises because some people will, unless restrained, cause harm to others. It will not do, then, to assume that those who work in government, whether as policymakers or civil servants, are somehow immune from self-interested impulses. The governance question is under what circumstances, in the presence of what institutions, will self-interest be directed to public purposes? Asking that question about a great variety of public issues ties together many of the activities of the Humphrey Institute.

The Institutional Design Perspective
at the Humphrey Institute

As a professional school with the tripartite mission of teaching, research, and outreach, the Humphrey Institute draws on both of the design perspectives. From a research perspective, it tries to identify institutions that are failing or are inadequate and to understand the forces that influence the direction in which institutions are evolving or create the need for new institutions.

In terms of resident instruction or teaching mission, the goal is to prepare individuals for productive engagement in public life. So the question of governance is this: How do a free people induce its members to behave in ways that accomplish public purposes? Institutional arrangements can be designed. At the micro level, for example, markets can be designed to perform more efficiently and equitably, government employees can be paid for results, and outcomes can be measured—all of which can orient and provide incentives for individuals to act in ways that accomplish societal beneficial outcomes. At the macro level, regulations and incentive systems can be designed that induce individuals to reduce environmental degradation, and adjustment policies can be designed to facilitate the adjustment to international trade.

Social and economic developments have also influenced the way entities such as the Humphrey Institute understand their work. Changes in resource endowments, cultural endowments, and technology have been important sources of institutional change in the past. Now three pervasive technological revolutions—in transportation, communication, and information technology—are driving institutional change in the United States and in the world at large. Collectively, they have dramatically lowered costs and significantly increased the scope of markets.

With increased openness, national governments begin to lose sovereignty. The corollary is that some part of policymaking and implementation shifts up to the international level and becomes embedded in international institutions such as the World Trade Organization, the United Nations Environmental Program, and a host of regional integration arrangements such as the North American Free Trade Agreement and MERCOSUL. Other policymaking and implementation shifts downward to local and other subnational governments.

These trends not only alter but also increase the scope for institutional design and redesign. The uproar in Seattle in 1999 illustrates the extent to which the World Trade Organization and other international institutional arrangements have been neglected. And difficulties in devising ways of handling incomes policy or welfare programs when they shift down to the state and local levels are legion. Much attention has been given to the problem of reforming government at the national level, at least in the United States, but little attention has been given to problems associated with shifting functions of government from the national to the international and state and local levels.

Scope and Range of Activities of the Humphrey Institute

The Humphrey Institute, in keeping with its land grant tradition, is a graduate-professional school and research center with a threefold mission: to teach individuals ways to be productively engaged in public life, to invent better methods of governance through research and design, and to extend that knowledge to policymakers and the general public.

The Humphrey Institute is part of the University of Minnesota, which has great strengths in the agricultural sciences, the biological fields, the medical fields, the basic sciences, the various engineering fields, and the social sciences. In addition, the university has strong professional schools in management, law, medicine, and public health. These two important distinguishing features of the university are great strengths for the institute, which draws on them in shaping programs and mobilizing faculty to draw on them for programs.

As a collegiate-level professional program, with an academic dean rather than a director as the top administrative official, the institute began with two programs at the master's level, one in public affairs and one in public planning, the former being the dominant program. The institute now offers the following degrees with a range of concentrations offered under each:

Master of public policy, with seven concentrations: advanced policy analysis methods; economic and community development; foreign policy and international affairs; public and nonprofit leadership and management; science and technology policy; social policy; and women and public policy. Students in these programs are expected to be able to work successfully in public agencies at all levels of government, for interest groups and think tanks, for elected officials, and for businesses interested in public policy issues.

Master of urban and regional planning, with eight concentrations: land use and human settlements; economic development; housing, social planning, and community development; environmental and ecological planning; conservation; transportation planning; urban and landscape design; and planning process, design, and implementation.

Master of science in science, technology, and environmental policy, designed to provide education in the social sciences to students who already have some depth in the biological and natural sciences, or engineering.

Executive master of public affairs, a one-year degree program offered to mid-career professionals. Because of its attenuated nature there is less opportunity for specialization, as the degree candidates already have depth in some professional field.

Another important component of the institute's instructional program is offered through its Center for Reflective Leadership, a certificate program with an evening program of instruction taught for local residents and an international fellows program offered for full-time students. Both of these are mid-career programs. The international program helps to enrich the student mix. Some of these students take regular course offerings in the institute.

The institute is now beginning to offer undergraduate course offerings. In addition, it offers joint degrees with other units of the university. One of these, with the largest number of students, is with the law school. Another is with the School of Public Health in Hospital Administration.

The research and outreach or extension missions of the institute are discharged in large part through the multidisciplinary centers. Among the eleven such centers are the Center for Democracy and Citizenship, Center for Nations in Transition, and Center for School Change.

The institute also seeks to capitalize on the university's traditional extension service, which has offices in each of the ninety-two counties in the state. The extension service provides partial funding for a full-time person in the institute to develop programs with the institute faculty and fellows and link them to the ongoing programs of the service. The goal is to access a wider range of talent in the university than do more traditional extension services. The extension service also finances, through a competitive grants program, more specific extension or outreach programs in the state.

Decision Making About Programs

In an effort to be relevant to the emerging problems of society, the Humphrey Institute engages in an ongoing review of its teaching, research, and outreach programs. It seeks to make changes in the structure of courses and their content as the public debate and the issues of concern to society begin to change. At a more basic level, the structure of all three program components—instruction, research, and outreach—is determined by the tenured and tenure-track faculty. Moreover, it has been an important feature to recruit generalists rather than highly specialized professionals who cannot speak to the broad needs of society.

The program flexibility tends to be reflected in its senior fellows. The institute spends considerable time identifying people who can fill its needs. Candidates are asked to submit a proposal to the institute indicating what they propose to do. In most cases the dean reviews these proposals and assists in ensuring that they are focused on important problems and in proper form. They then go to a senior fellows review committee, which makes a recommendation to the tenure-track faculty, who vote on whether to offer a contract.

An important part of keeping the program relevant occurs in the institute's ongoing seminars and workshops. One component of that process is the periodic presentations by faculty on the scope of their work and the problems they are addressing.

Activities of the Institute

Descriptions of some of the programs provide a good overview of the range of activities of the Humphrey Institute.

Sasakawa Global 2000 Program in Sub-Saharan Africa. Sub-Saharan Africa is perhaps the part of the world encountering the most difficulty in achieving sustainable economic and political development. Dependence on institutions imported from other countries is part of the reason. In the case of agriculture, that has meant, for example, the importation of the World Bank's training and visit extension system from India and the land grant university concept from the United States. In both cases there was little design work in adapting these institutions to the local cultural, political, and natural resource endowments.

The Humphrey Institute has been participating in some of the required institutional design work for a period of years through a linkage with the Sasakawa Global 2000 program based at the Carter Center in Atlanta, Georgia. The Sasakawa Global 2000 program is a technology transfer program in sub-Saharan Africa designed to bring about a second green revolution on the subcontinent. It was initially formed around the agronomic genius of Nobel Peace Prize laureate Norman Borlaug, father of the miracle wheats; the political skills of former President Jimmy Carter; and the financial resources of the Sasakawa Peace Foundation.

The original concept was that Borlaug would provide the leadership for the transfer of new technology for the production of maize, a food staple in Africa; Carter would provide the political leadership to persuade national political leaders to implement appropriate policies; and the Japanese foundation would provide the financing for the program.

The program started with a primary emphasis on technology transfer. It became obvious, however, that more attention needed to be given to the design and evaluation of appropriate economic policies. Borlaug and Carter turned to the Humphrey Institute.

This project now has programs in twelve countries. The policy work has addressed a wide range of problems, mostly having to do with the design of more efficient and equitable policies. These include making the case for agricultural modernization as a cornerstone to economic growth and development, the evaluation of price incentives for producers that will encourage the adoption of new technologies (which has led to work on international trade and exchange rate policies), and the involvement of women in the development process and the importance of the household as the vehicle for economic assistance programs.

Eastern Europe. The institute's work in Central and Eastern Europe came about in a different fashion. In the 1990s, as the countries of Eastern Europe broke away from the Soviet Union, the challenges of institutional reform were legion. The need was to design and implement institutional arrangements that could help these countries shift from a centrally planned society to one organized around representative democracies and free markets. Institutions appropriate for a representative democracy and a market economy were imperative. In addition, the centrally planned societies of the region had sorely neglected environmental issues.

When changes occurred in Central and Eastern Europe, the institute was well positioned to propose and undertake a variety of projects. The first program began in 1991 and involved the development of a neoclassical economics program at the Warsaw School of Economics. In undertaking this program, faculty from the Carlson School of Management and the Department of Applied Economics of the University of Minnesota, together with Humphrey Institute faculty and fellows, collaborated with faculty at the Warsaw School to design new courses and new curricula and develop new teaching materials.

The development of a new generation of policy analysts was deemed critical to the future of Poland. So an effort was made to establish a modern school of management with the University of Minnesota's Carlson School of Management. These new educational institutions are regarded as critical to the continued development of the Polish economy and the strengthening of policy arrangements.

A second program involved the development of local institutions to address the serious and much neglected environmental problems in five countries in Central and Eastern Europe. Humphrey Institute personnel collaborated with resident instructors to help local citizens understand and analyze local environmental problems. Part of the program concentrated on the development of new local institutions to address environmental problems. There are now a number of these new institutions scattered throughout the five countries. Care was taken in the design and development of the new institutions to make them sustainable by developing local sources of financial support. In the process of designing and developing these research and educational institutions, the program developed a number of what were described as blueprints for an appropriate environmental policy for the countries of the region. These comprehensive designs of environmental policy institutions have been widely adopted in the region.

School Reform. Several members of the Humphrey Institute, including the current dean, have been at the forefront in criticizing the nation's public school system as a monopoly and as a bureaucracy (that is, an entity that receives lump-sum funding not necessarily related to the quality of its work or the satisfaction of its clients). In their research and writing, they have argued that this system, without systematic rewards or penalties for performance, has undermined educational advancement in the United States. They point out, for example, that despite a tripling in real expenditures per student in the United States over the past forty years, there has not been a corresponding increase in educational outcomes. They see this as a case of a maldesigned system and have begun developing alternative designs. A senior fellow, the director of the Humphrey Institute's Center for School Change, is one of the inventors of charter schools, a reform begun in Minnesota in 1991 that has now taken root in three dozen states. Humphrey Institute personnel have been designing charter schools, advising those who are starting charters, distributing foundation funds to those devising intraschool reforms, and conducting research on other institutional arrangements in which educators are held accountable for their work.

Program Integration Within the Institute. The Humphrey Institute's programs are rooted in three areas: policy analysis, public planning, and public management. The resident faculty and fellows of the institute are located in the public policy arena. However, the other two areas contribute importantly to the institutional design work of the institute. The potential of the public planning work, which until recently might better be described as institutional planning, has grown as a result of the establishment of a multidisciplinary program in urban and regional planning. That new program, which involves faculty from the departments of applied economics, political science, architecture and landscape architecture, and geography, brings with it the potential for an expanded program of policy research, but the emphasis will remain on institutional planning, an essential ingredient of institutional design and reform.

Conclusion

Ultimately the design of policy institutions involves the public and other organizations through which policy is implemented. The goal of the institute is to have an expanded program that addresses the management of those organizations. In a school as necessarily diverse and as respectful of academic freedom as the Humphrey Institute, it is not possible to subsume all of the research, teaching, and outreach under a single rubric. Still, we believe that institutional design is the most appropriate way to describe the bulk of the activities here. It is informed by contemporary theory on governance, broadly applicable to great questions of public policy, and useful in the public arena. We predict that this approach will come to characterize more schools of public affairs.

Reference

Ruttan, V., and Hayami, Y. "Toward a Theory of Induced Institutional Innovation." *Journal of Development Studies*, 1984, *20*, 203–223.

For Further Reading

Brandl, J. E. "How Organization Counts: Incentives and Inspiration." *Journal of Policy Analysis and Management*, 1989, *8*, 489–495.

Brandl, J. E. *Money and Good Intentions Are Not Enough: Or, Why a Liberal Democrat Thinks States Need Competition and Community.* Washington, D.C.: Brookings Institution, 1998.

Boyte, H. C., and Hogg, K. S. *Doing Politics: An Owner's Manual for Public Life.* Minneapolis, Minn.: Project Public Life, 1992.

Cheung, S., Murphy, M. E., and Nathan, J. *Making a Difference? Charter Schools, Evaluation, and Student Performance.* Minneapolis, Minn.: Center for School Change, Hubert Humphrey Institute, 1998.

Minnesota Association of Charter Schools and the New Twin Cities Charter School Project. *Charter School Handbook.* (2nd ed.) Minneapolis, Minn.: Center for School Change, Hubert Humphrey Institute, 1998.

Munnich, L. W., Jr. (ed.). *State and Local Economic Development Strategy Summit.* Minneapolis, Minn.: Hubert Humphrey Institute, 1999.

Peters, S. *Cooperative Education and the Democratic Promise of the Land-Grant Idea.* St. Paul: Minnesota Extension Service, 1996.

JOHN E. BRANDL *is dean and professor of the Hubert H. Humphrey Institute of Public Affairs at the University of Minnesota.*

G. EDWARD SCHUH *is the Regents Professor of International Economic Policy at the University of Minnesota and the Orville and Jane Freeman Professor of International Trade and Investment Policy at the Hubert H. Humphrey Institute of Public Affairs.*

INDEX

Adams, C., 10
Adams, T., 10
Aid to Families with Dependent Children, 81
Albany, New York, 76
Albert, C., 64
Altmeyer, A. J., 10, 11, 12
American Bar Association, Judicial Division, 21
ANCHoR (Automated National Client-Specific Homeless Services Recording System) project, 66, 70, 72, 74
Anderson, D., 76, 78
Annie E. Casey Foundation, 52, 58
Applied research, 72
Arthur D. Little Company, 67
Askew, R. O., 92
Atkins, C., 64

Banfield, E., 31, 32, 35
Barbara Jordan Memorial Forum on Diversity in Public Policy (Lyndon B. Johnson School of Public Affairs), 46
Bascom, J., 8, 9, 11, 13
Beard, E., 64
Benjamin, G., 79
Big Dig project (Boston), 67, 68, 72, 73
Block, R., 57, 60
Bluestone, B., 69, 74
Bogue, A. G., 12, 16
Borlaug, N., 106
Boston, Massachusetts, 54, 55, 63–74
Boston College, 70
Boston Globe, 68, 73
Boston Herald, 73
Boston Urban Observatory (John W. McCormack Institute of Public Affairs), 63
Boyd, D., 83
Bradford, C. P., 54
British universities, 9
Brookings Institution, 81
Brunger, E., 77
Bulger, W., 64
Burke, J. C., 85

California, 29
Capacity Inventory, 59

Capacity Study (Federalism Research Group), 83–84
Carstensen, V., 11, 16
Carter, J., 106
Carter administration, 42
Carter Center (Atlanta, Georgia), 106
Castro, F., 92
Center for Democracy and Development (John W. McCormack Institute of Public Affairs), 66
Center for Ethical Leadership (Lyndon B. Johnson School of Public Affairs), 45–46
Center for Legislative Studies (Nelson A. Rockefeller Institute of Government), 79
Center for New York State and Local Government Affairs (Nelson A. Rockefeller Institute of Government), 79
Center for Social Policy (John W. McCormack Institute of Public Affairs), 66
Center for State and Local Policy (John W. McCormack Institute of Public Affairs), 65–66
Center for Survey Research (John W. McCormack Institute of Public Affairs), 63
Center for the Effectiveness in Higher Education (Nelson A. Rockefeller Institute of Government), 85
Center for the Study of the States (Nelson A. Rockefeller Institute of Government), 79, 82, 83, 84
Center for Women in Politics and Public Policy (John W. McCormack Institute of Public Affairs), 66, 70, 74
Central Artery/Tunnel project (Boston), 67
Central Europe, 106–107
CGU. *See* Claremont Graduate University School of Politics and Economics
Chamberlain, T., 10
Chambers, A., 49
Chase-Lansdale, L., 54
Chelsea, Massachusetts, 65
Chicago, 49–60
Chicago Community Trust, 50, 52, 55
Chicago Innovations Forums, 59

111

Back Issue/Subscription Order Form

Copy or detach and send to:
Jossey-Bass Inc., 350 Sansome Street, San Francisco CA 94104-1342

Call or fax toll free!
Phone 888-378-2537 6AM–5PM PST; Fax 800-605-2665

Back issues: Please send me the following issues at $23 each.
(Important: Please include series initials and issue number, such as HE90.)

1. HE _____

_____

_____

$ _____ Total for single issues

$ _____ Shipping charges (for single issues *only;* subscriptions are exempt from shipping charges): Up to $30, add $5^{50} • $30^{01}–$50, add $6^{50} $50^{01}–$75, add $8 • $75^{01}–$100, add $10 • $100^{01}–$150, add $12 Over $150, call for shipping charge.

Subscriptions Please ❑ start ❑ renew my subscription to *New Directions for Higher Education* for the year _____ at the following rate:

U.S.	❑ Individual $58	❑ Institutional $104
Canada:	❑ Individual $83	❑ Institutional $129
All Others:	❑ Individual $88	❑ Institutional $134

NOTE: Subscriptions are quarterly, and are for the calendar year only. Subscriptions begin with the Spring issue of the year indicated above.

$ _____ Total single issues and subscriptions (Add appropriate sales tax for your state for single issue orders. No sales tax on U.S. subscriptions. Canadian residents, add GST for subscriptions and single issues.)

❑ Payment enclosed (U.S. check or money order only)

❑ VISA, MC, AmEx, Discover Card #_____ Exp. date_____

Signature _____ Day phone _____

❑ Bill me (U.S. institutional orders only. Purchase order required.)

Purchase order #_____

Federal Tax ID 135593032   GST 89102-8052

Name _____

Address _____

_____

Phone_____ E-mail _____

For more information about Jossey-Bass, visit our Web site at:
www.josseybass.com   **PRIORITY CODE = ND1**